Praise for *Repentance: The Meaning and Practice of* Teshuvah

"Widely known as a foremost Jewish voice in the field of ethics, Louis E. Newman now expands his purview to spirituality, and does so in his own masterful way: combining biblical and Rabbinic wisdom with sophisticated analysis, yet presented in a touching and straightforward manner that requires no prior theological expertise on the part of readers. Neither soppy and banal nor turgid and technical, Newman appeals to our own intuitions and experience, to establish a specifically Jewish approach to an all too human predicament."
— **Rabbi Lawrence A. Hoffman, PhD**, editor, *Who By Fire, Who By Water*—Un'taneh Tokef and *The Way Into Jewish Prayer*

"A compassionate, nuanced guide, useful to laypeople and scholars alike, who seek to understand how the practice of repentance can bring healing to individuals and to the world."
— **Vanessa L. Ochs**, associate professor of religious studies, University of Virginia; coeditor, *The Book of Jewish Sacred Practices: CLAL's Guide to Everyday and Holiday Rituals and Blessings*

"Reveals the inner workings of a profound Jewish tool for personal transformation.... Bringing scholarship to the personal, this honest book both humbles and inspires hope in the same breath. Reading it, I felt my heart was purified."
— **Alan Morinis**, director, Mussar Institute

"A gem—for spiritual seekers and for all people interested in living a moral life. Combines the clear thinking and elegant prose of a fine scholar, the lucid presentation of a master teacher, and the richness and honesty of a thoughtful human being engaged in his own deep, ongoing work of *teshuvah*. A must for the serious Jewish bookshelf."
— **Rabbi Amy Eilberg**, co-founder, Yedidya for Jewish Spiritual Direction

"Throughout this very well-written book one truth resounds: Feeling fully alive requires a lifelong dedication to amending past hurtful actions, restraining harmful impulses, and always cultivating the fundamental goodness of our hearts so that we manifest the divine potential of loving compassion that is our birthright."

—**Sylvia Boorstein**, author, *Happiness Is An Inside Job: Practicing for a Joyful Life*

"A revelation…. Reminds us that we need not wait until Yom Kippur to think about how we transgress and what we need to do to redeem ourselves. Reading [this book] could change how we live, helping us to take the deep wisdom of Yom Kippur into our daily lives."

—**Rabbi Rebecca Alpert**, associate professor of religion and women's studies, Temple University

"This enlightening exploration of the moral, spiritual and interpersonal dimensions of *teshuvah* provides a rich introduction to Jewish texts and traditions alongside stirring insights from humanistic psychology. Newman goes beyond providing a wonderful work of scholarship to give us a moving guide to personal transformation. Powerfully addresses a contemporary moral challenge."

—**Rabbi David Teutsch, PhD**, Wiener Professor of Contemporary Jewish Civilization, Rabbinical College; director, Levin-Lieber Program in Jewish Ethics

"Dr. Newman's fine study of *teshuvah* is as impressive academically as it is personally moving. Drawing from a deep well of Rabbinic and theological sources, he manages to circumscribe the difficult topic of sin and personal transformation without ever sounding 'preachy.' I believe this is because the author speaks from his own humble experience. He invites the reader along on a courageous spiritual journey and we enter the heart of this religious and ethical ideal together. This book reinvigorated my faith—in my capacity to change and in God's active partnership in that process."

—**Rabbi Tirzah Firestone**, Jungian therapist; author, *With Roots in Heaven: One Woman's Passionate Journey into the Heart of Her Faith* and *The Receiving: Reclaiming Jewish Women's Wisdom*

REPENTANCE

REPENTANCE

The Meaning & Practice of *Teshuvah*

DR. LOUIS E. NEWMAN

FOREWORD BY RABBI HAROLD M. SCHULWEIS
PREFACE BY RABBI KARYN D. KEDAR

For People of All Faiths, All Backgrounds
JEWISH LIGHTS Publishing
Woodstock, Vermont

Repentance: The Meaning and Practice of Teshuvah

2010 Hardcover Edition, First Printing
© 2010 by Louis E. Newman
Foreword © 2010 by Harold M. Schulweis
Preface © 2010 by Karyn D. Kedar

For information regarding permission to reprint material from this book, please mail or fax your request in writing to Jewish Lights Publishing, Permissions Department, at the address / fax number listed below, or e-mail your request to permissions@jewishlights.com.

Library of Congress Cataloging-in-Publication Data

Newman, Louis E.
  Repentance : the meaning and practice of teshuvah / Louis E. Newman ; foreword by Harold M. Schulweis ; preface by Karyn D. Kedar.
    p. cm.
  Includes bibliographical references.
  ISBN-13: 978-1-58023-426-9
  ISBN-10: 1-58023-426-7
  1. Repentance—Judaism. 2. Sin—Judaism. I. Schulweis, Harold M. II. Kedar, Karyn D., 1957- III. Title.
  BM645.R45N49 2010
  296.3'2—dc22
                                        2009050413

10   9   8   7   6   5   4   3   2   1
Manufactured in the United States of America
Jacket design: Jenny Buono

Published by Jewish Lights Publishing
A Division of Longhill Partners, Inc.
Sunset Farm Offices, Route 4, P.O. Box 237
Woodstock, VT 05091
Tel: (802) 457-4000   Fax: (802) 457-4004
www.jewishlights.com

To all those
who have accompanied me on the
path of repentance,
for sharing with me their experience,
strength, and hope,
with gratitude and love.

Rabbi Abbahu bar Ze'era said, "Great is repentance, for it preceded the creation of the world, as it is said, 'Before the mountains were brought forth.... You say, "Turn back [repent], children of man"' (Psalm 90:2–3)."

Genesis Rabbah 1:4

Israel is redeemed only by means of *teshuvah*.

Maimonides, *Mishneh Torah*, Laws of Repentance 7:5

Repentance cannot be comprehended rationally; it does not really make sense. Even the angels do not understand what repentance is.

Rabbi Joseph B. Soloveitchik

Contents

Part VII: *Teshuvah*: Its Moral and Spiritual Meaning   177

Foreword
The "Yet" of *Teshuvah*—Turning

D r. Louis E. Newman's work is not a book about books. Its sources are not drawn from quotations and citations of others alone. His insights derive both from deep reading and deep living, from knowledge by description and knowledge by acquaintance. As Newman notes, one of the translations of the word *teshuvah* is "response." *Teshuvah*, in Hebrew, means an "answer." But an answer without a question is foolhardy and irrelevant.

To do *teshuvah*, I must first grapple with the question that haunts me as it haunted the Rabbinic imagination. The Rabbis postulated that God went on creating many worlds and destroying them, until the birth of this world (Genesis Rabbah 3:7). Even after God's latest creation, God grew disillusioned with the nature of humankind. It "grieved Him at His heart, and God repented that he had made man" (Genesis 6:6–7). God, as it were, was caught in a double bind. If God so willed it, humankind could be created flawlessly, imprinted with infallible moral perfection, and incapable of transgression. But such a creature would lack the freedom to accept or reject, to obey or disobey, divine commands. To create a perfect being without freedom would be to form an automaton. God's is the dilemma of parenthood: to give birth and cultivate a perfectly obedient child or to empower the child with the courage to say no. It is a risk to grant power to unpredictable humanity.

After the Flood, after the discovery that the human heart is "evil from [its] youth," God re-parented (Genesis 8:21). The divine parent no longer held the illusion of a humanly perfect child. God learned that the human being, for all its promise, is brittle, errant, forever stumbling over the block of sinful temptation.

But the Hebrew Bible and its Rabbinic commentary insist that human sin is neither original nor omnipotent. "Sin couches at the door; its urge is toward you, Yet you can be its master" (Genesis 4:7). This "Yet" is the promise of *teshuvah*, the faith in the human possibility to re-create, rebirth, and realize the potential in the divine image buried within the human being. Nature, human, and nonhuman, is now understood to be imperfect. Still, the "wheat can be ground, the lupine soaked, the bitter herbs sweetened, and the human being perfected" (Midrash Tanhumah, *Tazri'ah*)—perfectible, but not perfect. Without the "Yet" of human mastery, the human being is caught beneath the grinding wheels of inertia and fate.

According to a Rabbinic intuition, seven things were created *before* Genesis. Among these seven was what spurs Dr. Newman's insight that there is a reservoir of moral energy to respond to failure, to turn the self around (Babylonian Talmud, *Berakhot* 54a). It is that which we call *teshuvah*, without which the human being cannot grow nor civilization endure. It is a precondition for human moral survival. *Teshuvah* is hidden within the heart of the divinely imaged human being and its energies engage a stunning revolutionary collegiality between the two creative forces: God and humankind.

The dynamic interrelationship is foreshadowed in the very syntax of God's declaration in the Bible: "Let us make the human being, male and female, in our image, in our likeness" (Genesis 1:26). Who is the "us" that is referred to in this resolution? The "us" refers to no celestial powers, angels, or deities. "Let us" entails a singular Divine-human partnership, the seeds of potential awaiting moral actualization: God in and through the human being.

Unlike other creatures, the human being is not formed by divine fiat: "Let the waters swarm with living creatures ... let there be cattle ... " (Genesis 1:3, 30, 34). God calls for the joint effort with the human being to shape and refine the moral being. It is noteworthy that only with the human creation does the Bible use the two verbs "create" and "made" together (Genesis 1:26–27). This confers upon humankind the awesome capacity to engage. With this energy, the human being is raised to the heights of accountability and responsibility.

More than a static being, the human being is a constant becoming. *Teshuvah* celebrates the competence and capacity and courage to overcome, to change, to grow, to begin and begin again.

Still, a caveat is in order: Nothing is perfect, not even *teshuvah*. *Teshuvah* has its limitations. Narrowly focused on the self, *teshuvah* may easily slip into spiritual egoism. So it is told of the disciple who confessed to the Sage, "I try so hard to atone. I try to wrestle with temptation. I try but I do not succeed. I remain mired in the mud of transgression. Help me to extricate myself from sin and to truly repent." The Sage answered, "Perhaps, my dear friend, you are thinking only of yourself. How about forgetting yourself and thinking of the world?" (Martin Buber, *Hasidism and Modern Man*, p. 162).

Teshuvah begins with the self, but it must not end there; it would be only half a prayer. *Teshuvah* is neither divine grace segregated from human works nor human works amputated from the arms of grace. What begins as the solitary search within the self evolves into sanctification of our world.

Every little gain in this dynamic interplay of all the strands of our being overcomes the pessimism of Ecclesiastes: "Only that shall happen which has happened, only that occurs which has occurred" (1:9). *Teshuvah* is part of the great quest of re-creation. It is to explore the deepest self and to emerge newly "self-fashioned," able to declare, *"ani acher,"* "I am another." After entering into this book, you will not be the same.

Rabbi Harold M. Schulweis

Preface
Our Human Capacity for Change

Our story is shaped by a mysterious cacophony of successes and failures, chance and circumstance, talent and luck, friend and foe, doors that have opened and doors that have closed. As we witness and reflect upon our lives, we relive our significant moments over and over. In doing so we give emphasis, definition, and meaning to past events and ultimately to our lives. We can choose to focus on the negatives or the positives. Choice becomes the greatest power we have. We can choose to interpret challenging moments—some, the result of our having made bad choices—as if we are victims of conspiracies to cause our downfall. Or, we can see them as lessons which have shown us our inner strength, our resolve to aspire and persevere, our power to choose differently next time and affect a different outcome. This retelling—this returning—to events and people creates a persona of who we are in the present and who we can become. Therefore, the way we react and relay, and ultimately make sense of our story, illustrates the power of interpretation and perspective. We must believe in the human capacity for change.

Yetzer is Hebrew for the "creative force of the universe" and is described by the Rabbis as going in two directions: one good and one bad. As creatures created in the Divine image—both human and godlike—we carry with us this creative force and have the ability to transform any moment into good or evil, compassion or disdain, through its influence. Imagine *yetzer* as a power at the core of your being, like a powerful waterfall rushing through you. This force is both spirit and humanity, both present and potential, in constant motion. It is the consistent potential to elevate life and living.

Everything we are is subject to the shifting of our *yetzer*. Even our character traits, those characteristics essential to who we are, are not absolutes, affected as they are by our choices and the formidable call of our good and evil. Take, for example, the trait of self-confidence. Self-confidence, three degrees toward the dark, is arrogance. Self-confidence, three degrees toward the light, is leadership. It is up to us which direction we choose.

Teshuvah is *yetzer*'s correction, a path that returns us to center. It returns us toward light when our choices have led us into darkness. It is the acknowledgment of the spiritual potential within to either depress or elevate the human condition. Once upon this path, we are invited—again and again—to embark upon a journey of goodness and kindness, of righteous and ethical living. When we return to the center we are only three degrees away from living in the light of aspiration, where we can imagine and become who we were meant to be.

Repentance: The Meaning and Practice of Teshuvah is an important companion on the path to understanding our *yetzer*, our capacity for personal change, and our ability to shape our life's perspective. Dr. Louis E. Newman informs and enlightens our understanding of *teshuvah* by gently leading us through the texts of Jewish tradition, helping us learn what is required of us to harness the power of our creative force for good, and what to do when we veer in the wrong direction. In a voice that is personal and hopeful, he bravely shares his own experiences with *teshuvah*, illustrating how we too can transform our lives as our Rabbinic teachings would have us do. This book is not a memoir or a self-help book, it is at once a serious and human treatment of what we all seek—the return to our center. Whatever our past, we can choose new life. Despite our fear, we can have hope. Whatever wrongs we have committed, we can repent. We must believe in the human capacity for change, and this book shows us how.

Rabbi Karyn D. Kedar

Acknowledgments

I began working on the subject of repentance many years ago and it would be impossible for me now to properly thank all those whose insights have made their way into this book. I do, however, wish to acknowledge those who have had a direct hand in bringing this work into print. First, I am grateful to Stuart M. Matlins, publisher; Emily Wichland, vice president of Editorial and Production; and the entire staff at Jewish Lights for their encouragement and extraordinarily professional handling of all aspects of the publication process. They have been a pleasure to work with. I am indebted to Carleton College for granting me a sabbatical in 2008–9, which gave me the time to write the initial draft of this book. For twenty-seven years, Carleton has been my professional home and I have benefited immeasurably from the constant friendship and support of all my colleagues. I also appreciate the outstanding work of Hal Edmonson, Carleton class of 2009, who served as a research assistant for me on this project.

I have been privileged to be a member of two extraordinary spiritual communities that have nourished my soul over many years—Beth Jacob Congregation and my recovery fellowship. Whatever I know about *teshuvah*, beyond what can be found in books, I have learned from all those in each of these communities who have listened to me, challenged me, and encouraged me. Without them, this book could never have been written.

Finally, and most important, to my family:

My wife, Amy, has been my model of a life devoted to spiritual growth and profound self-awareness. Her support of my work and her guidance in my life have sustained me year after year. Her love is an immense blessing in my life.

My children, Etan, Jonah, and Penina, bring me more joy than I could ever have imagined possible. Their willingness to tease me about my shortcomings, but also to embrace me in spite of them, has enabled me to do my own work of *teshuvah*.

I know that I will never be able to express fully the depth of my love or the extent of my gratitude, but I hope that they will receive this book as a small token of my devotion.

Introduction
Exploring *Teshuvah*

Teshuvah (repentance) constitutes a central—some would say, the central—religious-moral teaching of Judaism. It is also the most pervasive and important—perhaps also the most challenging—problem of moral life for all of us. We cannot understand the ethics of Judaism without attending closely to what the tradition says about *teshuvah*, and we cannot understand our own moral situation, or improve our moral stature, without engaging in repentance. The goal of this book is both to clarify a key aspect of Judaism and to illuminate a highly significant aspect of our moral experience. In this sense, I hope that this exploration of *teshuvah* will be useful to people beyond the bounds of the Jewish community, for I believe that Judaism's wisdom about repentance can speak to people in all times and places.

It has long been recognized that *teshuvah* represents a central religious-moral category in Judaism. It is through repentance that we acknowledge our moral failings, repair our relationships with others, become reconciled to God, and return to the proper path. Jacob Neusner, the preeminent contemporary scholar of Rabbinic Judaism, has written:

> In Judaism, the conception of repentance—regretting sin, determining not to repeat it, seeking forgiveness for it—defines the key to the moral life with God. No single component of the human condition takes higher priority in establishing a right relationship with God, and none bears more profound implications for this-worldly attitudes and actions; the entire course of a human life, filled as it is with the natural propensity to sin, that is, to rebel against God, but

1

comprised also by the compelled requirement of confronting God's response, punishment for sin, takes its direction, finds its critical turning, at the act of repentance, the first step in the regeneration of the human condition as it was meant to be.[1]

Ehud Luz, a contemporary professor of Jewish thought, puts it more succinctly: "*Teshuvah* is a central concept in Jewish religious literature, and may be said to express the essence of the religious and ethical ideal of Judaism."[2] To explore repentance is to enter the heart of what Judaism teaches about our ongoing quest to live morally with others and to maintain our connection with God.

Yet, for all that has been written about the centrality of *teshuvah*, its many dimensions have rarely been clearly teased apart. To do justice to the complexity of the concept of *teshuvah*, we must delineate the multiple roles it plays in the religious and moral lives of traditional Jews and explore the theological underpinnings of the concept, as well as the practical and psychological results of living a life in which *teshuvah* is regularly practiced. It is one purpose of this book to explore these questions, to lay bare as much as possible what is entailed—psychologically, morally, and spiritually—by the idea and the practice of *teshuvah*.

If this task has not been systematically undertaken by contemporary Jewish thinkers and scholars of Jewish ethics, it is perhaps because the concept of *teshuvah* is so multifaceted. For we cannot discuss *teshuvah* without looking into the nature of the soul and its relationship to God, the nature of sin and the "evil inclination," the religious goals of moral life, its psychological dynamics, and its anchoring in a system of ritual practice. Accordingly, this investigation of *teshuvah* will touch upon many wide-ranging and difficult questions:

- How do we understand the very meaning of the Hebrew word *teshuvah*—as "turning," "returning," or "responding"—and what are the implications of those different metaphors?
- What aspects of human nature account for our immoral behavior, and to what extent can we overcome them?

- What are the effects of our transgressions—on ourselves, on others, and on our relationship with God—and how can we rectify them?
- What roles do remorse and guilt—often called the "moral emotions"—play in our moral development, and how can they be cultivated without paralyzing us?
- Are there transgressions for which repentance is impossible, and if so, why?
- What does it mean that God "calls us" to *teshuvah* and that God has created us for the purpose of repentance?
- What are the component parts of "doing *teshuvah*," and how are they interrelated?
- To what extent do we undertake the work of *teshuvah* ourselves, and to what extent does God facilitate it?
- What is the experience of *teshuvah* for those who engage in repentance continually throughout their lives?

In short, any study of *teshuvah* encompasses religious anthropology, moral psychology, theology, and, of course, ethics. The tangled web of thorny issues helps explain why many would choose to avoid the subject altogether.

Yet, we do so at our peril. Our moral integrity, our wholeness as persons whose lives include an irreducibly moral dimension, depends on our understanding of and engagement with repentance. After all, to repent is to engage in moral self-assessment, to acknowledge our misdeeds openly to ourselves and especially to those we have hurt, and to undertake a process of rectifying the wrongs we have done. Indeed, true repentance, as we will see, involves not only undoing the immediate effects of specific transgressions but also a far-reaching moral transformation, becoming a different sort of moral person, the sort of person who would not commit similar wrongs in the future. Repentance in the fullest sense, then, encompasses regret, apology, and restitution—the behaviors most often associated with it—but also a profound healing of our moral selves and our relationships with others. The complexity of repentance, and the difficulties we frequently encounter when we attempt it, reflect precisely how essential it is to our moral lives.

I have chosen, however, to exclude any extended discussion of forgiveness, even though in many people's minds *teshuvah* is immediately associated with forgiving others for the wrongs they have committed against us. This is because repentance and forgiveness, though closely related, are quite separate. Repentance is the task of the person who wrongs another person; forgiveness is the task of the person who has been wronged. Much has been written about the experience of forgiveness—whether it is psychologically possible, whether it is religiously required, whether it is done primarily for the benefit of the one who forgives or the one who is forgiven, and especially whether it should be conditional upon the repentance of the offender. All these questions, important and compelling as they are, are set aside here in the interest of pursuing a fuller understanding of repentance itself.[3]

To understand *teshuvah* in this sense, we will need to attend to both the theoretical and practical aspects of the subject. On the one hand, I explain the meaning and purpose of *teshuvah*—the religious beliefs about God and humankind and the relationship between them that make *teshuvah* both necessary and possible. On the other hand, I attend to the mechanics of *teshuvah*—how we accomplish it, what obstacles we face, and how we overcome them—the *halakhah* (law) of *teshuvah*. Finally, I consider the ways in which this whole tradition of teaching about repentance can have value to all of us today—Jews and non-Jews alike—who do not subscribe to the beliefs that originally gave rise to the concept and practice of *teshuvah*.

Outline of the Book

Given the complexity of the subject and the range of issues to be explored, I know of no systematic way to organize everything there is to say about *teshuvah* in Judaism. It will not do to separate out the theological, moral, and psychological aspects of *teshuvah*, for doing so would necessarily entail doing violence to an organically interrelated set of issues. Nor can we simply proceed through the source materials chronologically, as if the key to understanding *teshuvah* could be found by tracing its historical development. Instead, I have attempted to expose the inner logic of *teshuvah* without at the same time imposing structures that obscure the interconnections among issues. Accordingly, this investigation of *teshuvah* will proceed in several parts: sinfulness and transgression (part 1); atonement and expiation from sin (part 2); the process of doing *teshuvah* (part 3); the psychological, moral, and spiritual dimensions of *teshuvah* (part 4); the particular virtues that are needed for doing *teshuvah* (part 5); the obstacles that arise for those engaged in *teshuvah* (part 6); and finally, the deeper moral and spiritual meaning to be found in a life devoted to *teshuvah* (part 7).

I begin by examining the nature of human sinfulness, considered behaviorally, attitudinally, and existentially. It is a commonplace among contemporary Jews that sin is not a major preoccupation in Judaism (as it supposedly is, by contrast, in Christianity). But nothing could be further from the truth. From biblical times onward, Jewish thinkers have been deeply concerned with the problem of why we sin, the effects that our sins have, and the ways in which we can undo those effects. In part 1, I consider what Jewish authorities have taught about both the nature of sinfulness and its effects—the harm it brings to the individual, to society, and to the relationship between the individual and God. I also reflect here on the deeper meaning of sinfulness as a fundamental disorientation, a failure to relate ourselves properly to others and to God, and in the final analysis, a failure to be the sort of creatures we were created to be.

Part 2 turns to the many ways in which sins can be rectified. Although misdeeds once committed cannot be undone, they can be atoned for. Over the centuries, Jewish authorities have insisted that there are many ways to be cleansed of our wrongdoing; fasting, ritual sacrifice, the Day of Atonement (Yom Kippur), suffering, and death all effect expiation for our sins. In exploring each of these, we come to a richer understanding of why it is necessary and how it is possible to free ourselves from the taint of our transgressions.

Teshuvah is the name the Rabbis gave to the entire process of "turning back" as a moral and religious response to transgressions. In part 3, I spell out the several steps in this process as it has generally been described in the classical sources. Although various authorities delineate these steps somewhat differently, "doing *teshuvah*" entails accepting responsibility, feeling remorse, verbal confession, restitution, soul searching, and finally, refraining from a repetition of the offensive behavior. Each of these steps contributes something distinctive to the process of repairing ourselves and our relationships insofar as they have been damaged through our moral failings.

Next we need to consider the distinctive psychological, moral, and spiritual dimensions of *teshuvah*, to the extent that these can be teased apart. In part 4, I note the ways in which *teshuvah* operates on all these levels simultaneously. *Teshuvah* is a complex concept precisely because it requires us to transform our relationship to ourselves, to others, and to God. Indeed, as we will see, this multidimensional quality of *teshuvah* explains to a significant degree just why it is, in Luz's words, "the essence of the religious and ethical ideal of Judaism."

Part 5 identifies the distinctive virtues that are cultivated by penitents through the process of *teshuvah*: honesty, humility, and hope. Soul reckoning (*cheshbon hanefesh*) requires rigorous honesty, owning our own moral brokenness entails profound humility, and imagining and then striving to become a more moral person necessitates hope, sometimes even in the midst of moral despair. As we explore these aspects of *teshuvah*, we will discover that honesty, humility, and hope are all prerequisites for the work of *teshuvah* as well as the fruits of cultivating the practice of *teshuvah*.

Teshuvah sometimes encounters obstacles, both internal and external, that would seem to make it impossible. The people to whom we need to apologize may have died or be inaccessible to us. The very idea that we can repent and "clear our record" may be morally offensive, insofar as it undermines both our motivation to be good and the requirement that we pay the price for our transgressions. In part 6, I address what Judaism has taught about several such impediments to the process of *teshuvah*.

In part 7, I explore the meaning and value of living a life devoted to *teshuvah*. Through the ongoing practice of *teshuvah* we develop a new perspective on life that radically alters our relationships to others and to God. Through *teshuvah* we come to know our lives as marked by both radical responsibility and radical freedom, as products of our past yet capable of forging a new future

for ourselves. On the moral plane, *teshuvah* facilitates moral transformation and the healing of our relationships with others. On
the religious plane, *teshuvah* entails seeing ourselves "as God sees
us," with complete honesty, and cultivating the godly within ourselves, even redeeming the evil inclination that God has
implanted within us by turning its power toward greater goodness. The conclusion of the book, "*Teshuvah* in Our Time," suggests how and why *teshuvah* continues to be relevant to us today.

These are vast and complex issues. Given the nature of these
questions and the sheer volume of material within Jewish sources
that pertains to them, I could not possibly provide here a definitive
treatment of repentance. Doing so is both beyond my competence
and beyond the scope of any single volume. My far more modest
goal is to highlight key perspectives within Judaism on *teshuvah*,
both in theory and in practice. This is but an introduction to *teshuvah*, one that I hope will accurately reflect the range of the tradition's teachings on the subject and engage readers in their own
reflection on the meaning and value of repentance.

Exploring *Teshuvah* Academically and Personally

I approach this examination of *teshuvah* as a historian of Judaism
with a long-standing interest in Jewish ethics. Yet, in this set of
reflections I also hope to speak to those who have engaged in the
arduous work of repentance or who hope to. Both the scholarly
and personal dimensions of this work, and the relationship
between them, require some further comment.

These reflections are written from a historical perspective that
understands the tradition as evolving and complex, encompassing
multiple and sometimes discordant voices. There is no single
Jewish view of *teshuvah*, as there is no single authoritative view of
any other aspect of religious or moral life. My goal here is to identify and explore a range of different perspectives within Jewish
tradition on repentance, to see the ways in which they reflect
diverse beliefs about God, humanity, and the relationship between
them. Many previous discussions of "repentance in Judaism" have
tended to synthesize different views within the traditional sources
on the subject and as a result have distorted as much as clarified
the traditional teachings.[4] The operative metaphor for historians of

a religious tradition should be the weaving of a tapestry in which each thread is separate and distinctive, worthy of study in its own right, but also contributes to the larger patterns that emerge only when we take in the whole of the tapestry. I strive always to remain attentive simultaneously to the diversity and distinctiveness of the individual threads, and to the contribution that each makes to the tapestry as a whole. I recognize that the tradition comprises many different ideas and perspectives, but that the meaning of each can be fully appreciated only in relation to the greater whole. You should not be surprised, then, to discover as you read these reflections that there are contradictions and tensions among the viewpoints presented.

Among these reflections you will also find that I have drawn upon numerous disciplines, from biblical studies and theology to psychology and moral development, in addition to ethics. It would have been simpler to restrict the focus of this study to the ethical dimensions of *teshuvah*. But this approach would fail to do justice to the very richness of our subject. Indeed, *teshuvah* is fascinating and worthy of sustained attention precisely because it intersects with so many different aspects of our lives—our emotional and psychological needs, our development as individuals but also our responsibilities to society, our moral concepts and religious beliefs. If this examination of *teshuvah* is eclectic and even diffuse, I understand that as the price we must pay to grasp, even in broad outline, the nature and practice of repentance.

The complexity of the subject also accounts for the rather unconventional style of this book. Rather than attempt a linear or systematic analysis of the subject, as you might expect, I have chosen to explore the topic through a series of short, interrelated reflections, mini-essays as it were. This reflects in part my inability to produce a systematic account of repentance out of the multiplicity of sources and perspectives that Judaism provides. But it also mirrors the nature of *teshuvah* itself, the ways in which it is embedded in a web of meanings that do not readily lend themselves to linear analysis. Each short reflection begins with a text that points to one aspect of our topic, though exploring that theme or issue frequently leads into discussions of other texts and questions that are addressed in other mini-essays that appear either earlier or later in the book. This way of exploring *teshuvah* has something of the quality of a Talmudic discourse, which, like the term for "tractate" (Hebrew, *massechet*, literally "web"), mirrors the organic interconnections among a cluster of related concepts and issues.

This "web" of reflections is meant to help us trace the many threads of argument, the many themes and ideas, that weave their way through the tradition's treatment of *teshuvah*. Some of these threads will recur many times throughout these reflections, just as the same short statement may appear several times in the pages of the Talmud, in different contexts, but always pointing us to the interrelationship of many seemingly diverse topics. Like a Talmudic discourse, these reflections will incorporate various genres—philosophical analysis, textual exegesis, and narrative. Indeed, frequently a Talmudic discussion is interrupted by a story, an episode, that both illustrates something about the issue under discussion and helps bring the otherwise abstract debate back to the realities of lived experience. Here, too, I occasionally weave into the discussion some stories (real or fictional) of repentance, which I hope will supplement and elucidate the classical sources. Finally, and perhaps most significantly, this set of reflections is Talmudic in that it does not presume to offer firm conclusions. Like so many Talmudic discourses, this one offers many questions, together with multiple perspectives on the pertinent issues. It will point to ways in which the many dimensions of *teshuvah* are interrelated without offering fixed judgments about the "right" way to repent or the "best" theory of repentance. It is designed to open up, rather than close off, discussion of the subject. In precisely that sense, it aims to do what every Talmudic text does, namely, draw the reader into the discourse, as participant and interpreter.

This last point leads me to some final reflections on the academic and personal aspects of this study. I could have written an academic study of the concept of *teshuvah* in Judaism, designed primarily for those interested in a conceptual understanding of the topic. Indeed, when I first began work on this project several years ago, I assumed that this is precisely what I would write. But that would not have done justice to the truth of my own experience.

For, in addition to being a Jewish ethicist, I am also a penitent. Over the past several years, I have been a regular participant in a twelve-step recovery program, which, as all people in recovery know, is centrally about engaging in a "searching and fearless moral inventory of ourselves," "making amends," and reorienting ourselves to a "higher power." Twelve-step work, in fact, is all about doing *teshuvah*—recovering a sense of wholeness ("sanity"), restoring our relationships with others, and renewing our spiritual lives. To pretend that my interest in this subject was strictly academic would have been dishonest. It would have been similarly deceptive if I had written this book in two discrete sections, one part comprising an academic analysis of *teshuvah* and another part relating my personal views on the subject, which I briefly considered. But, on reflection, it became clear to me that the scholarly and personal parts of myself were not so neatly divisible. My scholarly reading of Jewish tradition on this subject has been colored by my personal experiences with repentance, and conversely, my personal struggles to repent have been shaped by my reading of the sources. To write this book in a way that suggested otherwise would have falsified my experience, both as a scholar and as a Jew engaged in repentance.

As a result, this book includes reflections, some of which are written in a more impersonal academic voice, others of which adopt a more personal tone. Both voices are authentically my own. This combination of styles, I hope, will make these reflections accessible to scholars and laypeople alike. For these reflections, taken as a whole, are meant to be both descriptive and suggestive, analytic and synthetic. That is why so much of what I have written here is cast in tentative language. This is not a matter of excessive false (intellectual) modesty but grows out of my desire to acknowledge the limits of my own certainty and to point to connections, name possibilities, and open this subject to readers. In this sense, the writing of this book is itself a part of my own process of "doing *teshuvah*," for it reflects my effort to honestly affirm my own commitments, to acknowledge my own limitations, to disavow any suggestion of pretense or of possessing more certainty than I actually have. And that is how it must be, for what could be the value of a book on *teshuvah* that did not exemplify the very qualities that the subject demanded?

So, I encourage you to read these reflections on *teshuvah* as an invitation to explore a rich tradition of discussion on these matters and to reflect on these texts in the light of the text of your own experience. In that way, your experience of reading these reflections will be consonant with my writing of them. For I have self-consciously examined *teshuvah* through the prism of my own experiences of sinfulness, guilt, and moral self-examination, of being called to account and of struggling to repent. In writing these reflections I have thus tried to mirror and extend the tradition's call to *teshuvah*. I hope that in confronting this tradition and my reflections on it, you will do the same.

Part I

The Nature of Sin

1

Dimensions of Sin

The LORD saw how great was man's wickedness
on earth, and how every plan devised by his
mind was nothing but evil all the time.

Genesis 6:5

If people were not subject to sin or prone to transgression, the question of repentance would never arise. Repentance is a response to sin, an effort to overcome its causes and undo its effects. It follows, of course, that to understand repentance in all its dimensions and manifestations, we must first attend to the nature of sin. Needless to say, this is a theological and philosophical subject of enormous complexity, and here we can only begin to explore some of its most basic aspects.

Sin is multidimensional and so can be considered from several perspectives. It is useful to distinguish these various aspects of sinfulness, even if in practice the distinctions among them are not as clear-cut as this analysis would lead us to expect. Still, we can helpfully begin by distinguishing the *behavioral, characterological,* and *spiritual* dimensions of sinfulness.

In the first instance, sin is about doing wrong. To transgress is to do what we should not have done (or, conversely, to fail to do what we should have). Many of our religious texts highlight this dimension of sin, as anyone who has read through the long lists of moral rules in the Hebrew Bible will readily recognize. "Do not steal," "Do not commit adultery," "Honor your father and your mother"—these are just a few of the most commonly recognized rules that dictate proper moral behavior. Transgress the rule

15

and you have sinned. In Hebrew, the most common word for sin is *chet*, meaning "to miss the mark," "to make a mistake." In this sense, the most basic element of sinfulness is behavioral, and people are more or less sinful depending on how frequently (and how egregiously) they fall short of accepted moral standards.

From this perspective, it is understandable that the traditional Jewish confessional prayers recited on Yom Kippur, the Day of Atonement, contain long catalogues of different sorts of sins. Of course, some commonly identified sins—covetousness, prejudice, and arrogance might be good examples—seem entirely interior and involve no observable act at all. But even from the behavioral perspective these can properly be regarded as transgressions either because they are "mental acts" or because these dispositions are so closely related to prohibited behaviors that as a practical matter they cannot be disconnected from them.

But sinfulness can also be seen as an element in human nature, rather than a trait of human behavior. It is more about who we are than about what we do. In this view, sin is much like ego, for it is an element that infuses our being. It may manifest itself in particular acts, but it cannot be reduced to them. For even if sin does not generate any particular misdeeds, it is there, latent within us. From this perspective, sin is akin to a virus or an inclination to behave in certain ways. We may only become aware of its existence when it bursts into the open and we notice its effects, but we should not confuse the effects of sin with its existence. It is very much a part of human nature, which is separable from the ways in which it affects our outward behavior.

Judaism acknowledges this sense of sin when it speaks of the *yetzer ha-ra*, "the evil inclination." Interestingly, the Hebrew word translated here as "inclination" is actually related to the word for creation. So, the phrase points to the idea that some part of us is innately evil, that we were created that way. This, like the passage from Genesis quoted earlier, may strike many Jews as alien to their understanding of Judaism. Christianity teaches the doctrine of original sin; Judaism believes that people are fundamentally good. Or so many Jews have been taught. But historically, Judaism has included teachings about the "evil inclination" that share at least a family resemblance to ideas about evil often associated with Christianity.

Finally, sin is sometimes thought of as a spiritual disorientation. Neither an act nor a character trait, sin is best understood as a relationship gone awry. A sinful person, in this view, needs to realign herself with the Source of goodness or truth, most often identified with God. Sin is a form—perhaps the primary form—of spiritual dysfunction. To be sinful, then, is to be alienated from God and in need of direction or renewed connection. It is a state in which we find ourselves when we become aware that we are disconnected from God. It is for this reason that many people speak of being "in sin," rather than of having "committed a sin" or having "a sinful character." The many Jewish prayers that invite God to help us turn away from our sins and back to God reflect this understanding of sinfulness.

Certainly these different views of sin are not mutually exclusive. Indeed, they can be related to one another in various ways. Some would point to misbehavior as just a symptom of sin, which is either a character defect or a broken relationship between the individual and God. Others, conversely, think of the sinful behavior as primary. The more we misbehave, the more we become habituated to sinning and the more we disrupt our relationship to the spiritual source of our lives.

How we think about sin may seem like a rather abstract, theoretical question. But nothing could be further from the truth. Sin is with us every day. It is as familiar to us as the traits of stinginess, arrogance, and prejudice that we recognize in ourselves. We encounter it daily when we lose our temper, belittle the achievements of those around us, or stretch the truth in order to make ourselves look a little better. It often shows up in the temptation to cheat or deceive others. And even when we resist that temptation, we recognize that the inclination to evil is active within us.

As you set out to explore *teshuvah*, you might well begin by reflecting on the ways in which sin manifests itself in your life. How do you experience your own misdeeds—as discrete missteps, as examples of deep-seated character flaws, or as spiritual failings? How and when are you most aware of your sinfulness? In what ways have you shielded yourself from the significance of your transgressions? What Judaism teaches about repentance makes sense only in response to the existence of sin and so can only be understood to the extent that you are ready to acknowledge and explore the reality of sin in your life.

2

Sin as Illness

Bless the LORD, O my soul
and do not forget all His bounties.
He forgives all your sins,
heals all your diseases.

Psalm 103:2–3

The analogy of sin to illness appears to be deeply rooted in Jewish tradition.[1] In addition to this quotation from Psalms, we find the following extended metaphor in Isaiah 57:19–21:

It shall be well,
Well with the far and the near—said the LORD—
And I will heal them.
But the wicked are like the troubled sea....
There is no safety—said my God—
For the wicked.

In what sense is sin like sickness, and what are the implications of this comparison?

Sin, like illness, is a natural condition. We become ill sometimes because our bodies fail to function normally. There are inherent weaknesses in our organs, as well as ways in which we are susceptible to germs and other environmental factors that assault our bodies from the outside. In much the same way, sin is an inherent weakness in our spiritual/moral lives. There are elements of selfishness, meanness, and even sadistic tendencies that exist within all of us and can be activated if given the opportunity. Sometimes a particular individual or situation tempts us, much as biological elements in our environment can take advantage of our inherent physical vulnerabilities.

Sin, then, is a natural condition. Just as no one would expect to go through life never falling ill, surely no one lives a sin-free life. But the good news in this is equally apparent. For the body has natural defenses against illness and injury. All of us have experienced the myriad ways in which our bodies can fight off diseases, regenerate skin that has been wounded, and sometimes even bring us back from the brink of death. Our souls likewise have regenerative powers that enable us to heal the self-inflicted wounds of transgressions we have committed or to restore our integrity after it has been compromised. Physicians often counsel us to "work with our bodies" as we recover from a physical ailment, and similarly the metaphor of sin as illness suggests that we have internal resources we can marshal in our efforts to repent.

Finally, like illnesses, sins can be more or less severe, chronic or acute, easy or difficult to heal from. There are sins that threaten to destroy our moral lives much as certain cancers endanger our physical lives. Other maladies, of the body or spirit, disrupt our lives only for a short time. But severe or mild, sins that we fail to attend to will eventually tear at our moral fiber and leave us weakened. This is undoubtedly why the Rabbis counseled us to "keep distant from a minor sin lest it lead you to a major sin" (Fathers According to Rabbi Nathan 5a). Maintaining our moral health requires constant vigilance and the cultivation of our natural defenses against sin, just as it is now widely recognized that physical health likewise is enhanced when we eat well and exercise regularly.

Thinking of sin as a form of illness—a moral and spiritual illness, as it were—cuts in two directions. On the one hand, we come to see transgressions as a natural part of living. Falling into misdeeds, like falling ill, is not in itself cause for alarm. On the other hand, staying healthy is an unending challenge, for there is no end to the ways in which we are vulnerable to disease and moral decay. And, notwithstanding the psalmist's praise of God as the healer of sin, it is evident that we have a certain degree of influence over the extent to which we are susceptible to this particular sort of illness. In this regard, the contrast between classical

Jewish and Christian teachings on sin is instructive. For many Christian thinkers, the operative metaphor for sin is death, not illness. Paul writes, "Therefore as sin came into the world through one man and death through sin, and so death spread to all men because all men sinned" (Romans 5:12). Sin as death is far more threatening to human life, so much so that the only remedy is a kind of salvation that involves conquering death, that is, resurrection.[2] Judaism, on the whole, would have us think of sin as less threatening, which leaves more room for and requires more cultivation of the practice of repentance.

So, let us imagine our transgressions as a form of illness—inevitable but remediable, threatening but not typically life-threatening—something to which we have a natural susceptibility but also for which we have natural defenses that can be strengthened.

3

Suffering *Shekhinah*

When man sins, he undermines the *Shekhinah*
[immanent aspect of God] and inflicts harm and
damage, as it were, on the Divinity itself ... when
one sins, one drives away the hapless *Shekhinah* who
suffers when a Jew sins. It is as if the sinner actually
harms the *Shekhinah* and inflicts a loss on her.

Rabbi Joseph B. Soloveitchik[3]

It is well known that in Judaism the transgressions we commit
against others are simultaneously offenses against God. Because
God is the source of the moral law, any violation of that law is by
definition disrespectful to the God who gave it to us. The Torah,
of course, is full of examples of God punishing individuals for
their transgressions against others: God exiles Cain for killing his
brother (Genesis 4:12), gives Miriam leprosy for speaking ill of
Moses's wife (Numbers 12), and punishes the Israelites for their
mistreatment of the poor (Amos 2:6ff., and throughout the
prophetic writings). But the idea that God is the enforcer of the
moral law still falls short of the claim that God actually suffers
when we sin. What does this mean, and how does it contribute to
our understanding of sin and repentance?

God depends on us for the fulfillment of God's plan for the
world. That plan involves making this earth a place where truth,
justice, and righteousness prevail, where there is peace between
nations, and where everyone acknowledges that all people have
been created in God's image. The blueprint for such a world, as it
were, is in God's mind, but the execution is up to us. God can pro-

vide us with the rules and even, in the classical view, reward and punish us as we comply with those rules (or fail to). But God is more than just a parent or judge who dictates what is right and metes out punishments when we do wrong. God's own fate is riding on our behavior, because the world we create is not merely a product of our choices—though it is that, to be sure—it is also the realm where God's presence either will or will not be realized.

The ancient Rabbis expressed this idea in the following striking midrash:

> "This is my God and I will glorify Him" (Exodus 15:2). When I acknowledge Him, He is glorified, but when I do not acknowledge Him, as it were, He is glorified merely in name. Similarly, you say, "You are My witnesses, says the LORD, and I am God" (Isaiah 43:12). When you are My witnesses, I am God, but when you are not My witnesses, as it were, I am not God.
>
> **(Sifre Deuteronomy 346)**

It is an extraordinary statement, perhaps even bordering on blasphemy. How could God's very existence depend on humankind's witnessing of it? Surely God's existence and glory must be independent of our recognition of them. The Rabbis' own language ("as it were") appears to reflect their awareness that they were on the verge of crossing a theological line.

But their viewpoint makes more sense if we refer back to a distinction they make in other places, between the *Ein Sof* (the eternal, transcendent aspect of God) and the *Shekhinah* (the indwelling, immanent aspect of God). That part of God that inhabits our world is, indeed, dependent on our recognition of it. The Rabbis frequently connect the *Shekhinah* with human activity, as when they say that God's presence dwells among us whenever two or more people gather to study Torah (*Pirkei Avot* 3:2) or when a judge issues a ruling in accord with the facts (Babylonian Talmud, *Shabbat* 10a). And, in reality, God's presence *is* manifest whenever we bring God's word or God's justice into our daily interactions.

Martin Buber expressed the same idea in his discussion of the Hasidic concept of letting God in:

> God's grace consists precisely in this, that He wants to let Himself be won by man, that He places Himself, so to speak, into man's hands. God wants to come to His world, but He wants to come to it through man. This is the mystery of our existence, the superhuman chance of mankind.[4]

We are not only God's servants, charged with performing particular tasks in the world. We are also extensions of God, in a very real sense the vehicles through whom God's own goodness becomes manifest in the world. God cannot feed the poor or clothe the naked but through our hands, and when we do these things, we are making divine compassion a reality.

Jews have long believed that our transgressions against one another have cosmic consequences. What is at stake in our moral interactions with others far transcends the effects that we can observe. When we hurt others, we not only affect them, but we also make this earth a place in which God's presence is less palpable to precisely that extent. This is the extraordinary opportunity and responsibility we have been given. When we choose wrongly, we not only disappoint God, or fail to do our divinely ordained duty, but we literally diminish the *Shekhinah*, driving it out of this world. Sins thus not only *offend* God, but they also *diminish* God.

4

Reverence for Sin

> May it be your will, our God and God of our ancestors, that you renew for us this month for goodness and blessing, and grant us ... a life marked by reverence for heaven and reverence for sin.
>
> **Prayer for Rosh Chodesh,**
> **the beginning of the new month**

"Reverence for heaven and reverence for sin" seems like a very odd pairing. Why should we have the same attitude to sin as we have to God? And what would it mean to have reverence for sin, anyway?

Reverence, especially in the Hebrew (*yirah*), suggests high honor, deference, and even awe. To revere sin, then, is to honor its power and to respect its influence in our lives. It is the very opposite of taking it lightly or minimizing the likelihood that it will hold sway over us. To understand why this is the appropriate attitude toward sin, we need to delve a bit into the ways that the Rabbis understood this element in human nature.

The Rabbis were keenly aware of the evil impulse in the human heart and repeatedly warned against succumbing to its calling. In many places they personify the *yetzer ha-ra*, "the evil inclination," and ascribe all sorts of devious qualities to it. Rabbi Simon ben Lakish, a third-century Sage, is quoted as saying, "The *yetzer* of man assaults him every day, endeavoring to kill him, and if God would not support him, man could not resist him" (Babylonian Talmud, *Sukkah* 52b). The idea of our sinful nature as something that threatens to kill us—and not just once, but daily—is meant to be a terrifying image. This impulse is so powerful, in fact, that Rabbi Simon ben Lakish imagines we would be powerless to defend ourselves from this assault were it not for divine intervention. The struggle with the evil impulse, then, is a matter of life and death, and the very persistence of this impulse is the first reason for us to respect its power in our lives. This view, of course, is somewhat in tension with the texts discussed earlier, where sin appears less ominously as a kind of sickness that is relatively manageable.

Yet if the evil impulse attacked us persistently but directly, we would perhaps be better positioned to defend ourselves. In fact, the Rabbis tell us, the impulse to do evil is wily and seductive. It may introduce itself to us as a modest traveler, then as a guest, and finally it takes over our home and makes itself master of the house (Babylonian Talmud, *Sukkah* 52a). In another analogy, the Rabbis compare the evil inclination to something that appears at first to be insubstantial, like a cobweb, but eventually becomes a thick rope that ensnares us and from which we cannot free ourselves (Babylonian Talmud, *Sanhedrin* 99b). These and similar metaphors reinforce the message that the evil impulse is devious and difficult to defend against. It catches us off-guard by masquerading as something much less threatening than it actually is. Anyone who has struggled to overcome an addiction surely recognizes the truth of this teaching.

In yet another insightful observation, the Rabbis suggest that the evil impulse knows how to find our weaknesses and takes advantage of them. If we are inclined to be charitable to others, it tempts us to give the money instead to our own family (Exodus Rabbah 36:8). If we are inclined to resist sinful behaviors, it will assure us that we can sin and rely on God's mercy to forgive us (Babylonian Talmud, *Chagigah* 16a). In these and other ways, the Rabbis tell us, we are prone to rationalizations to justify our transgressions, and this is itself part of how the evil inclination works to undermine our determination to pursue a righteous course of action in life.

No wonder, then, that the traditional liturgy includes many prayers imploring God to help us resist the evil inclination.

May it be your will, our God and God of our ancestors, that you ... not lead us into sin or transgression, nor into temptation or disgrace. Don't give the evil inclination dominion over us, distance us from evil people and bad companions, make us cleave to the good inclination and to good deeds, and bend our will to serve you....

(Traditional morning service)

The assumption behind these repeated pleas for assistance is the reality that resisting the *yetzer ha-ra* is enormously challenging. Only with the help of God, or what those of us in twelve-step groups refer to as "a higher power," can we overcome the seductive power of the evil within us.

This is hardly news to those of us who have looked deeply at our own tendency to do what we know we shouldn't. We cheat a little on our taxes because we convince ourselves that everyone does it, so we can, too. We pass off responsibility for our own mistakes onto others because we are afraid to accept the consequences. We turn our backs on those who need our support because we convince ourselves that what we have to give won't make a difference or, worse, that our financial support will make them dependent, and so we can feel righteous about our stinginess. In all these ways, we are susceptible to the power of the evil inclination precisely because it is so insidious.

Persistent, powerful, and devious—the evil inclination is a formidable adversary, indeed. Revering it entails an attitude of constant vigilance, knowing that, even when we have resisted it many times before, we may succumb at any point. It strikes many of us as old-fashioned, even downright medieval, to imagine ourselves each day in a pitched battle with the forces of evil within us. But the wisdom of this tradition is that we cannot make progress on the path of repentance if we underestimate the countervailing forces in our lives. Revering sin is the corollary of revering God, and the prerequisite for pursuing righteousness.

5

Sin, Guilt, and Impurity

Wash me thoroughly of my iniquity,
and purify me of my sin.

Psalm 51:4

What is the connection between sin and impurity? What experience of sinfulness lies behind this ancient cry to be cleansed of sin? And what does this metaphor of washing away iniquity tell us about the process of atonement and repentance?

When the prophet Isaiah imagines himself in the divine court in heaven receiving his commission to become a prophet, he immediately becomes conscious of his impurity:

I cried,
"Woe is me; I am lost!
For I am a man of unclean lips
And I live among a people
Of unclean lips;
Yet my own eyes have beheld
The King LORD of Hosts."
Then one of the seraphs flew over to me with a live coal, which he had taken from the altar with a pair of tongs. He touched it to my lips and declared,
"Now that this has touched your lips,
Your guilt shall depart
And your sin be purged away."

(Isaiah 6:5–7)

This vision reinforces the connection between sin and a sense of uncleanness or impurity. No one who stands before God—and certainly no prophet who would speak for God—can be unaware of his failings. In the presence of ultimate goodness and purity, Isaiah feels unworthy and in need of absolution from his sinfulness. The fire in the live coal symbolically burns away the sins of the past and enables him to begin his work as a prophet in a purified, guilt-free state.

In philosopher Paul Ricoeur's masterful study *The Symbolism of Evil*, he argues that the earliest consciousness of sin is of being unclean. He writes, "Dread of the impure and the rites of purification are in the background of all our feelings and all our behavior relating to fault."[5] At the most basic level, we sense that our transgressions leave a mark on us. We have dirtied our souls, soiled ourselves through our actions. The wrong we did is over, and there may be no record of it even in the memory of others (if it was committed in secret or without witnesses). But something in the transgressor has changed in a way that can only be described as analogous to a physical change. The sinner is tainted. And even if that residual mark is invisible to the naked eye, it is evident to those who feel the effect of their own transgressions as palpably as if it were seared into their bodies. This consciousness of sin as a physical mark on our bodies echoes down through the centuries to find literary expression in Shakespeare's *Macbeth* ("Will these hands ne'er be clean?") and in American writer Nathaniel Hawthorn's famous novel *The Scarlet Letter*.

This elemental awareness of sin as dirt and of atonement as cleansing runs throughout biblical literature. In Isaiah 1:18, the prophet announces:

Come, let us reach an understanding—says the LORD.
Be your sins like crimson,
They can turn snow-white;
Be they red as dyed wool,
They can become like fleece.

Even today, to be white is to be pure, free of taint. No doubt this accounts for the practice still observed by many Jews today of wearing a white *kittel* (robe) on Yom Kippur to symbolize their moral purity—or desire to achieve it. The biblical account of the Day of Atonement provides an elaborate purification ritual that presupposes this same notion of sin as a form of defilement that must be removed. Later I will comment on the details of the ritual in greater length; for now it is sufficient to note the verse that concludes and summarizes the whole ritual process: "For on this day atonement shall be made for you to cleanse you of all your sins; you shall be clean before the LORD" (Leviticus 16:30).

We are dealing here with a certain primal awareness of guilt as transgressing a moral boundary. In this most basic sense, the consciousness of sin is independent of the circumstances surrounding our misdeeds—whether we transgressed intentionally or unintentionally, flagrantly or hesitantly. These more subtle moral distinctions have their place in almost all systems of law and ethics, and they often affect the sort of sanctions that we feel should be imposed in response to this or that transgression.

But the experience of sin as taint arises at a more visceral level and reflects a more basic reality. Even if I was unaware of the moral prohibition, or was aware of it but transgressed it completely unintentionally, I transgressed all the same. The deed was done, and that objective fact cannot be changed. The clock cannot be turned back and the deeds we do cannot be undone. It follows that the process of cleansing relies on a divine force intervening from outside—a seraph with a live coal, a priest who sheds the blood of a slaughtered goat and sprinkles it about, or for Christians, the Crucifixion. Our deeds can mark us but not cleanse us of that mark, for we cannot unwrite the history we have written with our actions.

It is a long way from this concept of atonement to the view of repentance that comes to dominate in Judaism. There the intention of the transgressor makes all the difference, as does the intention and commitment of the penitent. There everything rests on the moral transformation of the wrongdoer, the penitent's self-awareness, remorse, acts of apology, and restitution. There the act of repentance can literally undo the prior act of transgression, suggesting, at least to some, a way of transcending the laws of causality. Yet, in the manner of all religions, earlier stages of awareness and more primitive rituals are transcended, but not erased, by later developments in the tradition.

The rituals of Yom Kippur—especially fasting, wearing white, and recounting the ancient rituals of expiation in the Temple—remind us that we all long to be cleansed, and we believe that that sort of expiation is still a possibility. We have long since left behind the slaughtering of the goat and the sprinkling of blood, the priest confessing the sins of the people on the goat and its being led into the wilderness. But on Rosh Hashanah we may stand by the edge of a river or lake and symbolically cast our sins away in the ritual known as *tashlich*. In an earlier generation (and even today, among the ultra-Orthodox) we find the practice of swinging a chicken over the heads of the children to magically transfer their sins to the animal, which is then ritually slaughtered. These symbolic gestures are remnants of that deeply engrained view that sin is akin to a physical mark that must be removed if we are to feel clean and morally upright again. And the very repetition of the words in the High Holy Day liturgy—"from all your transgressions before the LORD you shall be purified"—can become a kind of mantra, an incantation that also expresses our deepest hope that God will purify us, removing the stain on our souls and giving us a new lease on life.

The next time you become aware of having done something wrong, especially if it is serious, take a moment to notice where the sense of guilt resides in you. How do you experience it? How would you describe the sensation of feeling guilty? You may be surprised to discover that there is a tangible "something" that you sense as a kind of uncleanness. If you explore that feeling long enough, you will be well on your way to understanding why so many rituals of expiation involve symbolic acts of removal, cleaning, and purification. Perhaps you will even awaken to a desire to rid yourself of the sensation of guilt, to feel, in the prophet's words, "as white as snow."

6

Sin, Idolatry, and Truth

A company of liars cannot receive the Divine
Presence.

Babylonian Talmud, *Sotah* **42a**

Most of us think of idolatry as the worship of false gods. We
may bring to mind the famous midrash about Abraham
who smashed the idols in his father's shop as a way of challenging the belief that blocks of wood and stone could possibly be
divine. But religious thinkers have long recognized that idolatry is
actually a far more widespread and insidious phenomenon than
we generally suppose. Idolatry involves placing something non-
ultimate at the center of our lives, elevating it to a kind of "sacred"
status where it becomes the object of our devotion.[6] And many
have suggested that sin, when we examine it closely, invariably
turns out to be a form of idolatry in just this sense.

To see how this is so we need to get past the idea that sins are
simply transgressions of established moral rules. It is true, of
course, that violations of the Torah's commandments are regarded
as sins, and these are the particular behaviors that Jews atone for
each year on Yom Kippur. But this way of thinking about sin
doesn't help us see what makes any particular behavior sinful in
the first place. Consider what all those prohibitions—against stealing, lying, adultery, and the rest—have in common. From a spiritual perspective, the root of all these sins is living falsely,
representing ourselves in ways that are not true.

When we take what does not belong to us, we are pretending that we are entitled to something when, in fact, we are not.

32

When we commit adultery, we are lying to our spouses and breaking the sacred promises we made to them. Lying, of course, is the quintessential form of living falsely. But every form of treating others unethically—in the words of Hillel's famous maxim, treating others in ways that we ourselves would not wish to be treated—involves presuming that we have rights or privileges that we do not actually have. And in most cases, we do so knowingly and then devise some disingenuous justification to defend our indefensible behavior, which, of course, involves a second layer of dishonesty. Sin, then, invariably entails some form of living dishonestly, in a way that is at odds with the truth of who we are.

In a more explicitly theological sense, we could also argue that all sins are variants of the primary transgression, which is a failure to treat others as people created in the image of God. Negating that basic truth of human existence is at the core of all our misdeeds. For if we truly affirm that others are imbued with a spark of the Divine, and we act accordingly, we could not engage in any of the hurtful behaviors that are catalogued in those lists of sins that we're all so familiar with. It was this insight that no doubt led Augustine to affirm boldly, "Love, and do what you will."[7] For if we genuinely love God, and so love all God's creatures, we will always align our will with God's will, and so behave in ways that are righteous.

Sin, then, is about pretending that something is true when, in fact, it is not. Idolatry is pretending that something is divine and worthy of our devotion when, in fact, it is not. Sin and idolatry go hand in hand. Sin, we must conclude, is a kind of spiritual mistake, the result of being spiritually disoriented.

When we honor the truth about ourselves, embrace it and avoid any attempt to alter it in order to elevate ourselves above others or make ourselves look better than we really are, we are living with integrity. That is the moral description of truthful living. Religiously speaking, we are living piously, in connection with God, who is ultimate Truth. If I try to cover up or distort my behavior—that I lied to my boss, say, or gossiped about a friend behind her back—then in that moment I have abandoned the truth and I am engaged in a kind of idolatry. Because at that point

I have put the preservation of my reputation or image or good feelings about myself above commitment to the truth. And, as we have seen, making something other than truth the object of my devotion is a form of idolatry.

Doing *teshuvah*, turning away from sin, is all about choosing God over idolatry, truth over deception (including self-deception). All that is required is a fearless, unwavering commitment to truth—both about our individual lives and about human life in general. It is about refusing to pretend that we are more powerful, more entitled, more invincible than we really are. It is also about refusing to hide—from ourselves and from those we have hurt—the truth of what we have done.[8] To place truth and honesty at the very center of our lives, continuously and courageously, is the very opposite of idolatry. It is to worship what is genuinely ultimate, unconditional, and unchangeable.

This is the sort of life that the psalmist had in mind when he wrote:

> Who may ascend the mountain of the LORD?
> Who may stand in His holy place?—
> He who has clean hands and a pure heart,
> who has not taken a false oath by My life
> or sworn deceitfully.
>
> **Psalm 24:3–5**

Purity of heart and deed is equivalent to devotion to God, and this is a source of blessing and salvation. A similar message is embedded in a passage from the *Zohar,* a thirteenth-century mystical text, that has found a prominent place in the traditional Torah service:

> I am the servant of the Holy One, blessed be He. I bow at all times before the majesty of His Torah. Not in mortals do I trust nor in angels do I rely, but only in the God of Heaven who is the God of truth, whose Torah is truth, whose prophets are truth, and who abounds in deeds of goodness and truth. In Him do I put my trust and to His holy, honored name do I utter praises.
>
> (*Zohar, Parashat Vayakhel*)

When we acknowledge that our first and only allegiance is to truth, then we have turned away from idolatry in all its forms. We are ready to commit ourselves to a life of integrity. We are prepared to do *teshuvah*, and so we are open to hearing words of Torah.

Part II

Release from Sin

7

Between Two Absolutes: God's Demands and God's Forgiveness

The holiness of God thus creates both the consciousness of sin and the consolation which
makes the consciousness of sin bearable.
Reinhold Niebuhr[1]

There is something paradoxical at the heart of Western religious thought. On the one hand, God is presented as utterly demanding, holding humankind to moral standards that permit no compromise. On the other hand, God is said to be all love and forgiveness, ready to wash away our sins and offer us salvation. Some have even suggested that these conflicting views of God demonstrate the essential incoherence of Western theism. God cannot be both all demanding and all forgiving. But if we look more closely, we will see that these two seemingly contradictory views are actually complementary, and the relationship between them illuminates the nature of repentance and its place in religious life.

The God who demands absolute obedience of us appears at the very outset of Genesis, where God first gives Adam and Eve a prohibition ("as for the tree of knowledge of good and evil, you must not eat of it" [2:17]) and then banishes them permanently from the Garden of Eden when they disobey. In later biblical texts the divine demand is expressed even more starkly: "You shall be holy, for I, the LORD your God, am holy" (Leviticus 19:2). In the

Gospel of Matthew, early Christians amplified this demand yet further: "You, therefore, must be perfect, as your heavenly Father is perfect" (5:48). This leads naturally to the view that we are deeply flawed creatures in relation to the God who created us. This idea receives its most powerful expression in the liturgy for Yom Kippur:

> O LORD, before I was formed I had no worth, and now that I have been formed, I am as though I had not been formed. Dust am I in my life; even more so in my death. Behold I am before You like a vessel filled with shame and confusion. May it be Your will, O LORD my God and God of my fathers, that I sin no more....
>
> **(Traditional High Holy Day prayer book, morning service)**

But the contrary view asserts itself just as persistently. God is absolutely forgiving, even of the most die-hard sinner, for God's mercy and grace are infinite. The quintessential expression of this in Jewish liturgy comes in the recitation of the attributes of God, drawn (with some editing) from Exodus 34:6–7: "The LORD! the LORD! a God compassionate and gracious, slow to anger, abounding in kindness and faithfulness, extending kindness to the thousandth generation, forgiving iniquity, transgression, and sin." In the same Yom Kippur liturgy that emphasizes our sinfulness, we find these expressions of divine forgiveness:

> Almighty God, enthroned in mercy and governing Your people with loving-kindness, You cause their sins to pass away one by one. You are ever ready to extend Your pardon to sinners, and forgiveness to transgressors, judging charitably all the living, and not requiting them according to the evil they do.
>
> **(Traditional High Holy Day prayer book, morning service)**

And, of course, the prophetic literature is likewise full of expressions of God's boundless love for Israel and willingness to forgive even their most egregious transgressions.

> Who is a God like You,
> Forgiving iniquity

And remitting transgression;
Who has not maintained His wrath forever
Against the remnant of His own people,
Because He loves graciousness!
He will take us back in love;
He will cover up our iniquities,
You will hurl all our sins
Into the depths of the sea.

Micah 7:18–19

The conflict between these two views of God creates an inescapable problem in our moral lives. On the one hand, if God's moral demands of us are absolute and uncompromising, then we are doomed to moral condemnation. Our attempts to meet God's moral demands are doomed from the start, and so we might well conclude that the attempt itself is futile. Given the infinite distance between God's perfection and human imperfection, there is no possibility of being morally right with God.

On the other hand, if God's love and forgiveness are assured from the start, then we can sin with impunity and take refuge in divine salvation. God's forgiveness threatens to undermine human morality at its very foundation. Why be moral if in the final analysis we can throw ourselves on divine mercy? Surely I need not take my transgressions so seriously if I know that God will forgive them.

In short, in the first view, human justification is impossible; in the latter view, it is unnecessary. So, repenting for our transgressions is futile if we will always come up short, no matter how much we strive for moral perfection. And repenting is superfluous if we can always count on God's grace, no matter how much we fall short of human perfection. How are these two perspectives on God to be reconciled in such a way that there is both room for, and a point to, repentance?

For Jews, the doctrine of repentance plays the crucial role of mitigating these two conflicting perspectives. But here the sinner must take the decisive step (though, many would insist, this occurs with God's help). God's forgiveness of my transgressions is contingent on my willingness to acknowledge them, repair the damage I have done, and commit myself to avoiding those transgressions in the future; in short, divine forgiveness depends on human repentance. Through repentance, I confront my own moral failings and I simultaneously affirm the possibility of overcoming them and restoring a broken relationship with God, who reaches out to penitents in love. Repentance bridges the gap between the inevitability of moral failure and the assurance of divine forgiveness. Repentance thus simultaneously heightens my awareness of my sinfulness and unlocks divine forgiveness, for, as myriad classical Jewish sources insist, God forgives sinners as soon as they begin the process of repentance. In the words of one classic Rabbinic source:

> "Open to Me, My sister" (Song of Songs 5:2). According to Rabbi Yose, the Holy One said to Israel: My children, open to Me in penitence an opening as small as the eye of a needle, and I shall make an opening in Me for you so wide that wagons and coaches could enter through it.
>
> (*Pesikta d'Rav Kahana* 24:16)

The awareness of our sinfulness makes repentance necessary, and the awareness of God's forgiveness makes it worthwhile. Because God's moral demands of us are absolute and unwavering, we will always fall short and so always need to repent. And because God's love is abundant, our repentance, if it is genuine, is always met with forgiveness. This is surely one of the meanings of the oft-repeated teaching, "Great is repentance, for it turns a person's transgressions into merits" (Babylonian Talmud, *Yoma* 86b). The very same God who holds us accountable for our transgressions will also lovingly forgive us and judge us favorably. This is the power of repentance, which paradoxically enables us both to acknowledge our moral failings and to receive God's forgiveness.

8

Responsibility and Accountability

Know before whom you stand.
Traditionally written above the
ark, facing worshippers, in synagogues

Reflect on three things and you will never come to
sin: Know what is above you—a seeing eye, a
hearing ear, and all your deeds recorded in a book.
Pirkei Avot **2:1**

Implicit in the idea of sin and repentance is the prior concept of responsibility. Because I am a morally responsible agent, I am held to account for what I do (or fail to do) and so am in need of making right the wrong I have done (or, in another meaning of repentance, making right the person that I am). But what exactly is responsibility? Where does it come from, and what are its implications? Sorting out what we mean by responsibility will help us see how it is related to sin and so to repentance.

In its most basic sense, responsibility is attached to us as actors who say and do things that have effects on the world around us. If I drop a precious vase and it breaks, I am responsible for the damage. It was *my* action that resulted in the lost vase, and so I cannot avoid responsibility for what *I* have done. We come to understand this very simple sense of responsibility very early in life. All of us are familiar with the child who attempts to evade responsibility (and so the consequences that her parents or others might impose upon her) by claiming (often falsely), "But I didn't *do* it!" This is often followed by attributing responsibility for the fateful act to another person (younger siblings are often recruited to play this role). We know that if we didn't do the deed, we are not responsible for the consequences of that act.

Of course, we can commit an act and yet claim not to be responsible for our behavior. The Bible records such an effort to evade responsibility in the story of Adam and Eve. When God asks Adam, "Have you eaten from the tree about which I commanded you not to eat?" Adam responds, "The woman that You put at my side—she gave me of the tree, and I ate" (Genesis 3:11–12). The same tactics of evasion continue when God next confronts Eve: "What have you done?" to which she responds, "The serpent duped me, and I ate" (Genesis 3:13). Each knows that the quickest way to exoneration for the transgression he or she has committed is to displace responsibility to another agent. Yes, I did the deed, but others made me do it, or persuaded me to, and so I should not be held accountable. Needless to say, this sort of reasoning does not get them very far with God.

God doesn't cut them any slack here because it is understood that they each chose to eat the forbidden fruit of their own free will. They could have resisted, and it is precisely because they didn't that they are culpable. The point of the story is clear, as are its implications for responsibility: we are responsible for our behavior whenever we could have acted otherwise. It is our freedom to act (or not) that makes us responsible for what we do (or fail to do). This is the point that Maimonides makes about the relationship between culpability and freedom:

> This [the principle of free will] is a great principle and a foundation of the Torah and commandments, as it is written [in Deuteronomy 30:15], "See, I have set before you this day life and good, and death and evil" ... that is, the capability is yours, with respect to anything that a person wishes to do, whether good or evil ... accordingly, the Creator does not compel anyone, nor decree that one should do either good or evil, but rather everything is up to them.
>
> (*Mishneh Torah*, **Laws of Repentance 5:3**)

But responsibility presupposes more than just the freedom of the agent; something else is implied by this first story of sin and punishment. The moral command that defines human responsibility is absolute and unconditional. As the biblical scholar Walther Eichrodt observed:

> Here the obligation imposed by the Law is unconditional, and cannot be avoided by recourse to any other divine court of appeal more kindly disposed to human interests…. In the strict "Thou shalt" of the Decalogue and of other brief basic laws it is not some human lawgiver but the divine Lawgiver who speaks and makes His will the absolute norm.[2]

The Bible, in presenting moral commands as expressions of God's will alone, makes them inviolable. Adam and Eve do not have the option of appealing to some other authority, nor of questioning whether God's command really applies to them or not. They are not free to avoid responsibility by claiming that they are somehow exempt from this particular command at this time. Their responsibility is absolute, just as God's will is absolute, not subject to negotiation or compromise.

Finally, this religious view of human responsibility presumes that human behavior is visible. God sees us, knows what we have done, and calls us to account. This, too, is clear from that earliest biblical story, which records that Adam and Eve attempt to "hide themselves" in the garden when they sense God's presence (Genesis 3:8). Of course, this too is an unworkable strategy for avoiding responsibility. There is nowhere to hide, no place to put ourselves that is beyond God's ken. This further heightens the sense of human accountability, for even our most secret transgressions are not secret. Our responsibility for what we do is both unconditional and inescapable, for our moral duties derive from God and are enforced by God, who does not share this role with others, either human or divine. There is no possibility of evasion—not by dissembling, negotiating with, hiding from, or outliving the One before whom we are accountable.

Such a view of accountability is far removed from the one that prevails today among contemporary, secular (and even many religious) people. We regularly watch politicians and other public figures on the evening news, accused of some crime, proclaiming their innocence. In most of these cases, it emerges in time that they were, in fact, guilty of the crimes with which they were charged. But they believe—with some justification in our culture—that evasion is possible, that if they protest loudly enough and insist on their innocence persistently enough (and, especially, if they hire the best lawyers), they might just get away with it. What is strikingly lacking in all these performances (and it is hard to call them anything else) is that sense of absolute responsibility and accountability that is central to this religious view of human behavior. For what would be the point of proclaiming our innocence if we understood that we were guilty before God and subject to divine retribution for our transgressions?

It is in this context that repentance comes to have particular significance as the opportunity to affirm our responsibility and restore our integrity. Even in those cases where we might "get away with it" on the human level, indeed even in cases where no other person knows or could possibly discover our transgression, repentance still has its place. For the absolute responsibility we have before God is mirrored by the absolute opportunity to acknowledge our wrongdoing and receive release from the guilt that accompanies it.

When we begin to live our lives as if we stand continually before God, who sees us at all times, then we are ready to assume a kind of infinite responsibility for all our deeds. We are also ready to recognize our inescapable need for *teshuvah*.

9

Freedom, Fate, and Repentance

"The stranger need not lodge outside" (Job 31:32).
The Holy One declares no creature unfit—He
receives all. The gates [of repentance] are always
open, and he who wishes to enter may enter.

Exodus Rabbah 19:4

Throughout history and across cultures, people have been drawn to the idea of fate. Certain experiences, it seems, lead us to believe that there is something—a god, or perhaps a force of necessity to which even the gods are subject—that dictates the course of our lives. Things happen to us, especially painful or tragic things, and we are left feeling that they were destined, that we could not have avoided this misfortune. There is a shadow hanging over us, and we are powerless to control the effects it has on the course of our lives. At times, of course, fate is invoked in a happier sense, as when we believe we were fated to find the love of our lives when we serendipitously crossed paths in the unlikeliest of ways. But even when the results are favorable, the belief in fate stems from a deep-seated sense that there are powers in the universe that determine our destiny in important ways.

This idea of fate is closely connected to the classic debate about determinism and free will, which has preoccupied philosophers for centuries. On the one hand, it seems that the law of cause and effect requires that we see all events as determined by earlier events in the causal chain. Despite what we may believe, there can be no free will, at least not in any meaningful sense. On the other hand, our own experience leads us to feel that we do

47

exercise real choices, that we are free to choose a course of action, and that the future depends on what we do in the present, at least in most respects.

We need not delve into the intricacies of this debate, let alone attempt to resolve it, to see how these views shape an understanding of human freedom and so of repentance. If even some events in the future are fixed and immutable, then it is only reasonable to resign ourselves to the inevitable. To struggle against fate may be heroic, but it is ultimately futile. Indeed, much of the pathos of Greek tragedy derives from the ways in which the protagonists are unwittingly caught in a web of fate from which they cannot escape. Oedipus has been fated to kill his father and marry his mother, and no choices he makes can alter this horrible conclusion to the tale.

This tragic outlook on life is precisely antithetical to the view that gives rise to the idea of repentance. For if repentance means anything, it points to a radical human freedom, especially to the possibility of freeing ourselves from the effects of our own past transgressions. The past does not determine the future; our destiny is not fixed and beyond our power to change. No matter what we have done, we can make a decision to "turn" in a different direction tomorrow. In the most profound sense, no choice we made in the past is final or irredeemable, and even our most awful misdeeds can propel us in a radically new direction.

There are many implications of this idea of human freedom that I will address later in this book. But for now I want to highlight the ways in which this moral freedom is embedded in a still more general conviction that the world is conducive to our moral growth. As Jews have read in the biblical account of creation, the world is intrinsically "good," not only in the sense that it fulfilled God's expectations, but also in the sense that it has positive value. The natural world around us and the human soul that God breathes into us are both good. This doesn't mean that natural evils don't exist or that they don't matter. Earthquakes, storms, and disease afflict humankind, and the biblical writers were certainly not blind to the devastation they can cause. But none of this detracts from the fundamental conviction that the world, as the product of God's creative will, is good. Similarly, the Bible is

quite focused on the evil that we do—indeed, human moral failing and God's response to it could be said to be the central theme
of the Bible. But here again the irreducible goodness of human
life is generally assumed. It is this perspective that finds expression in the Rabbis' statement, which comes to have a prominent
place early in the traditional daily morning worship service,
"LORD, the soul that you have given me is pure."

It follows from this perspective that God has created us with
the potential to live righteously and has placed us in a world that
supports, rather than impedes, our moral striving. As the text of
Deuteronomy repeatedly reminds us, the good and evil that happen to us are responses to our moral choices. If we live a life of
righteousness, God will reward us with abundant sustenance and
peace, while if we stray from God's requirements of us, we will be
met with hardship and material deprivation. Most modern people
find these beliefs untenable. And, taken literally, they are. But
surely the point of the biblical author is really just this: the world
is designed in a way that it rewards our efforts to maximize our
innate goodness. Life is stacked—not against us, but in our favor,
in support of our desire to express our goodness and our efforts to
maintain right relationship with our Creator. When we do what
is good, the goodness of the world meets us and affirms our
choice. In the words of the prophet Isaiah:

> Seek the LORD while He can be found,
> Call to Him while He is near.
> Let the wicked give up his ways,
> The sinful man his plans;
> Let him turn back to the LORD,
> And He will pardon him;
> To our God,
> For He freely forgives.
>
> **Isaiah 55:6–7**

In such a world, there is no room for moral despair. The notion
that I am destined for some terrible fate or that the choices I have
already made condemn me to a future I cannot change is here
completely negated. I am free to choose against my own past, and

not only this, but God promises to meet me more than halfway when I do. Rather than resign myself to the blind forces of fate, or even to some iron law of causality according to which I cannot undo what I have already done, I can turn to the Jewish view of repentance, which affirms that we are free. And when we use that freedom to choose the path of righteousness, we are simultaneously expressing our truest nature and aligning ourselves with the goodness of the world as God created it.

10

Atoning through Sacrifice

It must be confessed that for *reflection* there remains something impermeable in the idea of ceremonial expiation, something that refuses even to be reduced to the richest symbolism of "pardon." What resists reductive reflection is the ritual *praxis* itself. This *praxis* is non-reflective by its essence.... That is why a catalogue of rites, such as that of Leviticus, remains in the end a mute and sealed work.

Paul Ricoeur[3]

In ancient times, the common way to be granted atonement for a sin, at least an inadvertent one, was to offer an animal sacrifice to God. A typical example of such a ritual can be found in Leviticus 4:27–31:

If any person from among the populace unwittingly incurs guilt by doing any of the things which by the LORD's commandments ought not to be done, and find himself culpable—once the sin of which he is guilty is brought to his knowledge—he shall bring a female goat without blemish as his offering for the sin of which he is guilty. He shall lay his hand upon the head of the sin offering, and the sin offering shall be slaughtered at the place of the burnt offering. The priest shall take with his finger some of its blood and put it on the horns of the altar of burnt offering; and all the rest of its blood he shall pour out at the base of the altar. He shall remove all its fat, just as the fat is removed from the sacrifice of well-being; and the priest shall turn it into smoke on the altar, for a pleasing odor to the LORD. Thus the priest shall make expiation for him, and he shall be forgiven.

We can set aside for now the complexities of the whole biblical system of sacrifice, which have occupied biblical scholars for generations. Our interest here is in the experience that underlies such rituals and in the theory of sin and atonement that they imply.

How does the sacrifice of an animal effect expiation? How would the participants in this ritual—both the sinner and the priest—have understood the means of atonement? What is the significance of the sinner's placing his hands upon the head of the animal before it is slaughtered, and what is the purpose of the priest's sprinkling of the blood of the animal in the ways he does?

Rituals of all sorts are notoriously opaque and multidimensional. Their power lies in the symbolic nature of the gestures, even as the meaning of those symbols is rarely made explicit. Moreover, a ritual can acquire new layers of meaning as it is revised and reinterpreted over centuries, some of which may be entirely unconscious even for the participants. In a ritual such as this, which involves sin and atonement, killing and burning and blood, we should beware of simple explanations that would reduce these powerful gestures to a single set of meanings. Let us begin by considering just a few of the possibilities that have been proposed by scholars. As we will see, each way of analyzing the meaning of the ritual has slightly different implications for the way we think about atonement.

It is possible that the point of sacrifice is first and foremost to appease the wrath of God toward the sinner. The logic of this is fairly straightforward: the sinner has insulted God through a transgression and now needs to offer God something of value as a way of placating God. There is a kind of quid pro quo here: God relinquishes the right to punish the sinner in exchange for the sinner's gift to God of an unblemished animal, which was a possession of significant value to the ancient Israelite worshipper. In a sense, the sin creates a kind of debt that can be repaid through the material sacrifice of the transgressor. Sacrifices are a kind of bribe, a way of paying God off for the offense caused by our bad behavior. There is something compelling in this way of approaching sacrifice, though it would not enable us to account for the elaborate rituals surrounding the gift of the animal.

Perhaps the most common theory of sacrificial atonement is that the animal slaughtered represents the sinner. As the famous anthropologist Edmund Leach put it:

> Before the sacrificial animal is killed, the donor of the offering invariably establishes a metonymic relationship between himself and the victim by touching the victim on the head. The plain implication is that, in some metaphysical sense, the victim is a vicarious substitution for the donor himself.[4]

In this view, the sinner himself is deserving of death, and both the severity of his guilt and his willingness to sacrifice himself to atone for his sin are represented vicariously by the sacrificial animal. By placing his hands on the animal before it is slaughtered, the sinner is saying, in effect, "You and I are one. I appoint you as my surrogate, and in offering you up for sacrifice, I am expressing my willingness to die to atone for my transgression [or, perhaps, I am killing the evil within me that performed this deed]." Viewed this way, the death of the animal atones because it symbolically represents the death of the sinner (or of the sin within the sinner), and so the donor emerges from the ritual cleansed. Turning the animal into smoke, literally making it disappear, magically transforms the status of the sinner, making him, too, disappear, and leaving in his place a purified individual. Talmudist Rabbi Joseph B. Soloveitchik articulates this view when he writes:

> In a world of strict justice, the only acceptable way is for man to sacrifice himself.... By sinning, he loses his most elementary right, the right to his own self.... When man brings a sacrifice after having sinned, he must imagine that it is he himself who is being offered upon the altar.... Repentance itself—that is the acquittal, the expiation. Repentance takes the place of the sacrifice of myself which I had a duty to offer upon the altar. It stands in my place and it is as if I myself were stretched out upon the altar.[5]

Others have suggested that sacrifice is not about vicarious death at all, but about communion with God. The French archeologist and biblical scholar Roland DeVaux suggested that the laying of the donor's hands upon the animal is not "substitutional," but merely a matter of identifying the owner and beneficiary of the sacrifice. The donor is saying, "This is *my* animal that *I* have brought as a gift to make atonement for *my* transgression." The animal is a gift to God, a way of demonstrating that the sinner has given up something of value to restore his good favor in God's eyes. It is also a kind of communal meal. God, after all, smells the "sweet savor" of the animal burning, and so, in a sense, the worshipper and God are sharing in the enjoyment of the sacrificial animal. This gift and shared meal restores the worshipper's close relationship with God, thus repairing the breach that was created by the transgression.

Still others have argued that the sacrifice here is meant to represent the inner transformation of the transgressor and so is intimately tied to penitence and remorse. According to professor and author John C. Lyden:

> Many people seem to view cultic sacrifice as a practice of superstitious primitive peoples who think that their gifts can placate the divine wrath or make up for their sins. Viewed as such, sacrifice indicates an amoral understanding of God's justice and human guilt. However, this interpretation misunderstands the nature and purpose of sacrifice. Primarily, it is neither propitiation of the gods' anger nor satisfaction for sin but a medium whereby the worshippers are related to the divine, a "ferry-boat between heaven and earth" ... sacrifice was understood as the ritual that symbolically connected them to their God.... Sacrificial acts show the penitence of the sinner and give concrete expression to his or her desire to repent.[6]

In this view, the key to understanding sacrifice is to recognize that the outward behavior is all symbolic of an inward transformation in the attitude of the donor. The gift of the animal is an empty gesture if it is not accompanied by the gift of the spirit, that is, by remorse and penitence. Of course, later Israeli prophets made exactly this point with respect to sacrifice:

I loathe, I spurn your festivals,
I am not appeased by your solemn assemblies.
If you offer Me burnt offerings—or your meal offerings—
I will not accept them;
I will pay no heed
To your gifts of fatlings....
But let justice well up like water,
Righteousness like an unfailing stream.

(Amos 5:21–24)

For I desire goodness, not sacrifice;
Obedience to God, rather than burnt offerings.

(Hosea 6:6)

It is not the animal sacrifice that effects atonement, but the inner change in heart that is represented by the gift of the animal. A similar point was made by Rabbi Soloveitchik:

> When a Jew brings a sacrifice for atonement, how are his sins expiated? Is it by virtue of a two-shekel lamb? Certainly not! Atonement comes to him through the recognition and confession of sin embodied in the act of sacrifice. This confession means abnegation and annihilation of self, total submission and subservience, sacrifice of self, of all one's being and possession ... as though one were oneself laid upon the altar.[7]

Notice how Soloveitchik draws on the idea of the animal as a surrogate for the sinner, but now only in an emotional sense, not as an actual vicarious offering. It is as though engaging in the sacrificial ritual is intended to raise the awareness of guilt and remorse in the worshipper and so bring him to that state of submission and self-sacrifice that are the hallmarks of genuine penitence and piety. Here the ritual sacrifice is but an impetus to spiritual transformation and a representation of it.

Jacob Milgrom, who has devoted much of his life to the study of Leviticus and related priestly documents, argues that the key element in sacrifice is the shedding of blood. The fact that this blood is wiped on the altar and spilled at its base is essential to the understanding of what is happening in the sacrifice overall. He argues that the inadvertent transgressions of the Israelites were understood to "cling" to the altar and to render it impure and unfit for offerings to God. So the point of the sacrifice is to "cleanse" the altar of the taint of sin, and this is done by blood, which is the essence of life and therefore purifying. Perhaps, too, the intimate connection between blood and life and God (the giver of life) means that blood contains a kind of divine power that is precisely what counteracts the human desecration of the altar. The underlying idea, then, is that sin is defiling and blood is needed to resanctify the altar so that it can continue to function as a place for worship of God.

Two different views of sin and its consequences can be discerned in these various ways of conceiving sacrifice. On the one hand, sin might be a relatively insignificant mistake, especially in cases like this, where the transgression was performed inadvertently. It is a debt that can be repaid, and when it is, the debt disappears. Alternatively, sin might be a very grave matter indeed, one that rightfully demands the death of the transgressor. Only the vicarious sacrifice of the animal and the symbolic destruction of the sinner/sin can purify the transgressor and restore him to God's good graces. As Ricoeur notes in the opening epigraph, we will never know precisely what was in the minds of the Israelites as they sacrificed their animals on that altar, how they understood their own behavior or the expiatory power of the rite.

But this much would seem to be clear: God provides Israel with the means to atone for its transgressions. This means that our transgressions, however serious, are not fatal. There is a prescribed way to restore a relationship with God after it has been severed by our misdeeds. As obvious as this may seem, this is not self-evident. We could easily imagine a God who was less forgiving and a notion of sin that permitted no redemption. But God is forgiving, and atonement is possible. Although the precise mechanism may be clouded in some obscurity, the fact that God provides a way back from transgression to purity and wholeness is striking and can only have been understood as an expression of God's love for Israel.

Finally, this sacrificial system would seem to be fail-safe. If we only perform the proper gestures, transfer the animal to the priest, who, in turn, reduces it to smoke and ashes before God, then our slate can be wiped clean. Of course, later prophetic and

Rabbinic teachers would insist that no ritual replaces the sincerity and inner remorse of the sinner, which alone makes all the difference. But the priestly system would appear to be more transactional and, if you will, mechanistic. And this is surely a source of comfort to ancient Israelites weighed down with a sense of their misdeeds. The path forward is clear, it has been prescribed; now it needs only to be followed and then our offenses disappear into thin air, along with the smoke of the sacrificial animal.

Like our ancestors before us, we need the reassurance that atonement is possible and that we know the mechanism for achieving it. In this light, we can begin to appreciate the enormous crisis that our ancestors must have experienced when the Temple was destroyed and the ancient sacrificial system became obsolete. Without a way of effecting atonement, the burden of accumulated sins would become unbearable.

It was the genius of the Rabbis that they appreciated this problem and provided a solution. It is a solution that has stood the test of time and continues to provide us with a way to overcome sin.

> Once as Rabban Yohanan ben Zakkai was coming forth from Jerusalem, Rabbi Joshua followed after him and beheld the Temple in ruins.
>
> "Woe unto us" Rabbi Joshua cried, "that this, the place where the iniquities of Israel were atoned for, is laid waste!"
>
> "My son," Rabban Yohanan said to him, "do not grieve. We have another atonement as effective as this. And what is it? It is deeds of loving-kindness, as it is said, 'For I desire mercy, and not sacrifice' (Hosea 6:6)."
>
> **(Fathers According to Rabbi Nathan 4)**

The moral deed has replaced the ritual deed; the loving gesture to another person substitutes for the gesture of slaughtering an animal. But the goal remains as important to our lives as ever. We live with the assurance that acts of sin can be counteracted by deeds of atonement.

11

Day of Atonement

For on this day atonement shall be made for you
to cleanse you of all your sins; you shall be clean
before the LORD.

Leviticus 16:30

Nowhere is the significance of sin and atonement more apparent than in the rituals prescribed for Yom Kippur, the Day of
Atonement. The very fact that ancient Israelites set aside a day
on the calendar to effect expiation for the sins of the people testifies to the utmost importance of purifying the people of their
transgressions. The rituals themselves are elaborate and, like all
rituals, remain rather opaque and open to multiple interpretations. Let us focus here just on the elements that seem most
prominent.

We begin by exploring the meaning of the word *kippur*, generally translated as "atonement". In its root, *k-p-r*, the word means
to "cover over," "rub off," or "wash away." From these very tangible gestures, the word seems to acquire the more metaphorical
sense of covering over transgression or guilt, or washing away our
sins. This in itself is instructive, for it reaffirms the sense that for
the Israelites the experience of sin and guilt was at least akin to a
physical stain. The rituals designed to achieve expiation, then, are
a sort of cleansing action. Indeed, as we will see, the use of blood
may be in part a reflection of their belief that blood was uniquely
suited to spiritual cleansing.[8] A secondary, but related, meaning of
k-p-r is to ransom or redeem a person, as reflected in the related
word, *kapparah*. This implies a different understanding of sin,

according to which the offense must be paid for, not merely erased. The offering of animal sacrifices detailed throughout the Torah (not only on the Day of Atonement) testifies to the belief that a transgression generates a sort of debt to God that must be repaid by giving up something of value. In this sense, the sacrifice is akin to our contemporary notion of paying fines for our offenses. Both *kippur* and *kapparah* play a role in the Day of Atonement.

One of the most striking aspects of the ritual involves the atonement for the altar. After describing the sacrifice of a bull as a sin offering, Aaron sprinkles some of its blood on the covering of the ark:

> Thus he shall purge the shrine of the uncleanness and transgression of the Israelites, whatever their sins; and he shall do the same for the Tent of Meeting, which abides with them in the midst of their uncleanness.
>
> **(Leviticus 16:16)**

The altar, it seems, absorbs the sins of the Israelites and so requires a yearly ritual cleansing. The blood of the slaughtered animals is assumed to purify the altar, perhaps because, as the Torah reminds us repeatedly, the blood is the life (see Leviticus 3:17, 17:14; Deuteronomy 12:23). If they recognized that the blood carries the life force within all living beings, that element that is most closely associated with divine power, then it is not surprising that blood would purify the altar of sin. Blood is the ultimate symbol of both life and death. It is imbued with the divine power that creates and sustains life, and the shedding of blood causes the death of the animal. To smear the horns of the altar with blood and to sprinkle blood all around are symbolically to destroy the old life of sin and to create life anew that is pure and free of taint. Of course, relinquishing the animal also represents a material gift, a financial loss that symbolically repays the debt to God incurred by the Israelites' transgressions. When the altar, that place where the people draw close to God through their offerings, is cleansed and their debt to God is repaid, then the holiness of the sanctuary has been restored.

The second element of the Yom Kippur ritual is, if anything, even more peculiar. A second goat, set aside for Azazel,[9] absorbs the sins of the people and is sent off into no-man's land.

> Aaron shall lay both his hands upon the head of the live goat and confess over it all the iniquities and transgressions of the Israelites, whatever their sins, putting them on the head of the goat; and it shall be sent off to the wilderness through a designated man. Thus the goat shall carry on it all their iniquities to an inaccessible region; and the goat shall be set free in the wilderness.
>
> (Leviticus 16:21–22)

A different sort of magic is at work here, one that relies on the power of words, rather than the power of blood. Confessing the sins of the people enables the priest to transfer them to the animal and then to banish them to a place of no return. It is as though putting the sins into words makes them tangible, so that the priest can actually place them on the head of the goat and physically remove them from the community.

These two aspects of the Yom Kippur ritual complement one another. The altar must be cleansed of sin, but so too must the community of Israelites as a whole. The former is accomplished through a ritual of bloodletting and purification, where the effective agent is nothing less than the divine energy contained within the animal's blood. The latter relies upon the use of language, which alone can externalize and concretize the guilt of the people and so turn the remaining goat into a vehicle for displacing the people's transgressions to a desolate place far, far away. Sin, the Torah is telling us, inheres both in the place where God dwells (the sanctuary) and where the people dwell (the community). The place of God's holiness must be cleansed, and the place where the community dwells must likewise be cleansed, by turning their sins into words that can be sent into exile.

It has been more than twenty centuries since these rituals of expiation have been performed, yet they continue to speak to us today about the power of sin and the means for expunging it. Sins have physical effects in the world that can only be reversed through physical acts that remove them. Although we no longer believe that slaughtering a goat and spreading its blood around is effective, nor do we confess our sins on the head of a goat and send it into the wilderness, we still recognize the ways in which transgressions alter our state of being. They "weigh on us" and "follow us" when we move from place to place. Yom Kippur reminds us that we cannot undo our transgressions in some abstract, ethereal way. Atonement is messy; it requires us to cleanse our lives, killing off one part of ourselves and giving birth to another. It demands that we take what is hidden in our hearts and verbalize it, so that in making it audible for ourselves and others we can place some distance between ourselves and the guilt that has plagued us.

And finally, Yom Kippur reminds us that none of this is undertaken alone. On this one day of the year we stand together in the courtyard of a Temple that stretches from one end of the earth to the other, believing that our collective deeds and unified voice have the power to remove our sins from us as a people. This is why the passage from Leviticus quoted earlier is written in the plural. We may each perform our own transgressions individually. But God takes account of our sin collectively, as a people. Only as a community can we approach God, purify ourselves, and begin anew.

12

Suffering Atones

Sufferings are beloved, for as sacrifices atone, thus
do sufferings atone. Sufferings have a greater
atoning power than sacrifices.

Sifre **32**

The idea that suffering has any positive value at all will strike most contemporary Jews as strange. The redemptive effects of suffering are frequently associated with Christianity, especially the doctrine that Christ's suffering and death on the cross were an offering that atoned for the sins of the world. Judaism, by contrast, is supposed to offer a more life-affirming attitude toward worldly existence. We think of suffering as undesirable and antithetical to living a spiritual life. If life brings us suffering, we may need to make our peace with it, but we certainly wouldn't praise such a life or seek it out.

But classical Jewish sources acknowledge that suffering can play a constructive role in life, and particularly in the life of the penitent. To understand why and how this is so, we need to consider what happens to us when we experience suffering.

Perhaps there has been a time in your life or in the life of someone close to you when you have known significant suffering—a life-threatening illness, a physical disability, or simply extreme discomfort or pain. Such experiences often force us to adjust our assumptions about life. A car accident may leave someone confined to a wheelchair and unable to work in the ways he once did. A stroke may leave someone unable to communicate with others and thus dependent on others for help in daily living.

Illness, pain, even significant discomfort can shift our frame of reference—our expectations about what life holds for us, our sense of personal power, and our relationships with others. In short, suffering of any sort forces us to confront our vulnerabilities, sometimes very dramatically. We are susceptible to debilitating disease, to accidents, to losing all the physical and mental capacities that seem to make life meaningful and enjoyable.

Coming face to face with our vulnerability is generally a psychological challenge, quite apart from the physical challenge of dealing with the actual pain or disability. It requires that we confront the uncomfortable fact that, like it or not, we are not the masters of our fate, at least not in many respects. Aware of our own frailty, we may ask fundamental questions about our lives: in light of this suffering, what is truly valuable about my life? Priorities that once seemed obvious to us we may now call into question. Our values may change when things that we have valued about our lives, and often taken for granted, are suddenly taken from us.

Suffering, especially if it is severe or long-lasting, almost inevitably humbles us precisely because it shakes us to our core, forcing us to reassess our values and adjust our expectations of life. In all these ways, suffering can be an inducement to the sort of soul reckoning that plays such an important role in *teshuvah*. Sin is closely related to an attitude of haughtiness or entitlement, a belief that the ordinary rules don't apply to us. Suffering undermines this attitude of arrogance and so makes us more receptive to acknowledging our moral frailty, as well. Of course, this is especially the case if the suffering we experience is causally related to the transgressions we commit, for example, if the car crash that left us injured was caused by our drunk driving.

These reflections help us see why someone might actively induce suffering in order to create the conditions that will facilitate *teshuvah*. But there is another kind of logic that links suffering and repentance. To suffer is to "pay" for our sins through a kind of sacrifice. By sinning, we gained something we were not entitled to—we inflated our own ego or improved our own position in someone else's eyes by maligning someone, or we avoided being penalized for something we did by lying about our involvement. Whatever the circumstances, we benefitted from our transgression and so we "owe" something. In a sense, the cosmic scales have been upset and now need to be righted. When we suffer, we pay the price for our wrongdoing. The penalty, in terms of lost pleasure, compensates for the wrongly gained benefit of our transgression.[10] Especially in an age when it was assumed that God punished people in very tangible ways for their sins, the experience of suffering was closely associated with the idea of paying for our sins.[11]

Finally, suffering might be understood as an outward manifestation of an inner transformation. Symbolic ritual forms of self-denial give penitents a way of making concrete, both for themselves and for the community, that they are actively atoning for their sins. Over the centuries there have been many such rituals—wearing sackcloth, fasting, and refraining from wearing jewelry, leather, or other adornments. These are outward manifestations of the remorse that the penitent feels, ways of giving tangible expression to feelings of humility and regret. Like many other religious rituals, these intensify the experience of engaging in a spiritually significant process and enable the penitent to share that experience with others in the community.

Whether naturally (or divinely) imposed or self-inflicted, suffering is a powerful way to be cleansed of wrongdoing. It facilitates soul reckoning, represents a tangible payment for transgressions, and is an outward expression of remorse. It makes us feel in our bodies the effects of transgression on our souls. Paradoxically, it is through such bodily deprivation that we gain spiritual wholeness and well-being. For if prosperity can lead to complacency and spiritual numbness, then suffering can lead to humility, introspection, and moral regeneration. In that light, it is no wonder that the Rabbis proclaimed, "Therefore, let man rejoice in suffering more than in prosperity," for it is suffering through which we receive pardon and forgiveness (*Sifre* 73b).

13

Death as Atonement

Let my death atone for all my sins,
iniquities, and transgressions that I
have committed before You.

From traditional deathbed confessional

When our lives are over, what becomes of our sins? Do they
die with us, or do they outlive us and continue to be held
against us? Because all of us sin and all of us eventually die, we cannot avoid the question of the relationship between the two. Given
our mortality, how shall we think about the longevity of our sins?

It appears that Judaism provides two different ways of viewing this problem. On the one hand, several sources indicate that
death puts an end to sin definitively. Sin is a category that applies
only to the living. In death, we are free of sin and free of its
effects. But even this position is subject to a number of interpretations, for death could cancel sin in several different ways.

First, if sinning is a product of our *yetzer ha-ra*, our evil inclination, then with our demise that inclination likewise ends. All
desires, both for good and evil, live in us and so die with us. Just
as the dead are not hungry or subject to any other kind of
appetite, they are also not subject to the inclination to do evil. As
one classic Rabbinic source puts it, "The evil inclination has no
power after death" (Genesis Rabbah 9:5). Given that death is the
end of everything, it logically must also be the end of sin.

There is another, more abstract sense in which death may
put an end to sin. To sin is to transgress, to fail to live up to our
obligations. But in death the whole concept of obligation to fulfill

the law is inapplicable. As the Talmud puts it, "When one dies, one is freed of the obligation of the law and its precepts" (Babylonian Talmud, *Shabbat* 151a). Whatever happens to us after we die, we are no longer in this world and so no longer subject to its rules. We escape from the realm of obligation—and so also of transgression—entirely.[12]

But on further reflection, it is clear that the relationship between sin and death may not be quite so easily resolved. For one thing, the Rabbis believed that the soul outlives the body, so the part of us that survives our bodies might well continue to sin or bear the burden of our sins. In addition, the effects of our sins could, and often do, outlive us. Our transgressions may originate in us, but they could be understood as having a "life of their own," which does not end just because our lives do.

This second, more complicated view of sin might be best understood if we think of sin as analogous to a kind of debt. If I owe my neighbor money and die before I repay it, the debt is not canceled, it is merely transferred to my estate. My heirs will have to make my neighbor whole. My obligation to my neighbor in this case outlives me. The point of a debt is that it involves the redress of some harm we have done or repayment of some benefit we have received. We owe something, and the people to whom that debt is owed are entitled to repayment whether or not I happen to die.

In this sense, our sins are the moral debts we owe to others. If I have benefitted by harming others, I need to make them whole. And if I am no longer around to do that, they need to be made whole all the same. Even if there is no monetary component to the transgression, and so no issue of restitution is involved, the obligation to apologize and seek forgiveness remains. Moreover, our sins continue to weigh on our relationship with God even after we die, for the soul, like God, is eternal. In this model, it seems that death does not put an end to sin.

It is this view, I think, that underlies the deathbed confessional cited in the opening epigraph. If sin is akin to a debt that will survive us, as we prepare to die we are acutely aware that we no longer have time to make restitution to those we have harmed or to reconcile ourselves to God. So we pray that our death will be accepted by God as satisfaction of all our outstanding debts incurred through a lifetime of sins. This final confession purifies the soul of the taint of sins not otherwise atoned for during our lifetimes and so allows us to die with a clean slate, so to speak.

Death puts an end to sin, then, either automatically or through a final confession whereby we ask that relinquishing our lives be regarded as payment for all the unfulfilled obligations that we have incurred through our sins. No doubt generations of Jews have found comfort in the knowledge that their sins would not outlive them. For if sin dies with us, then it is possible to attain in death what we could not find in life—complete freedom from sin.

Part III

The Way of *Teshuvah*

14

Turning: The Meaning of a Metaphor

Turn us unto you, O LORD,
and we shall return.
Renew our days as of old.[1]

Lamentations 5:21

It is a striking fact that the noun *teshuvah* does not appear anywhere in the Hebrew Bible. It seems that the full-blown concept of repentance as we know it is a later invention. Still, if we look closely, there are many passages that concern the idea of turning either away from God or back toward God. Throughout the Bible we find verbs that signify movement in relation to sin and atonement, and analyzing these gives us further insight into the earliest seeds of the concept of *teshuvah*.

There are several verbs in Hebrew that signify turning: *panah, sur,* and *shuv.* The first, *panah,* is related to the word for "face," and so suggests turning our gaze in a certain direction. Consider the following verses:

Yet I will keep My countenance hidden on that day, because of all the evil they have done in turning [*panah*] to other gods.

(Deuteronomy 31:18)

We all went astray like sheep,
Each going [*paninu*] his own way.

(Isaiah 53:6)

While to Me they turned [*panu*] their backs
And not their faces.

(Jeremiah 2:27)

In each case, the Israelites are described as having turned their backs on God. They look away toward other gods, and because they are oriented in the wrong direction, they are like sheep that have lost their way. And because they have turned away from God, it is not surprising that God "hides God's face" from them, effectively responding in kind. Here the verb suggests attentiveness, because we turn to face others when we want to pay close attention to them. So turning their faces in the opposite direction signifies that the Israelites are not looking to God, not aware of God's presence or attuned to God's commands.

A somewhat different metaphor is suggested by the verb *sur*, "to turn aside." Here a person is understood to be moving in a certain direction but then wavers or strays off course. Again, looking at some characteristic biblical usages is instructive.

And Moses said, "I must turn aside [*asurah*] to look at this marvelous sight; why doesn't the bush burn up?" When the LORD saw that he had turned aside [*sar*] to look, God called to him out of the bush.

(Exodus 3:3–4)

Let me pass through your country. I will keep strictly to the highway, turning off [*asur*] neither to the right nor to the left.

(Deuteronomy 2:27)

They have been quick to turn aside [*saru*] from the way that I enjoined upon them.

(Exodus 32:8)

You shall act in accordance with the instructions given you and the ruling handed down to you; you must not deviate [*tasur*] from the verdict that they announce to you either to the right or to the left.

(Deuteronomy 17:11)

What man is there who desires life, and loves many days, that he may see good? Keep your tongue from evil, and your lips from speaking deceit. Turn away from [*sur*]² evil and do good; seek peace, and pursue it.

(Psalm 34:13–15)

Unlike *panah*, which always has a negative connotation, *sur* is neutral. Swerving off a predetermined course may be a positive thing (if what distracts you is the miracle of a burning bush) or a negative thing (if it draws you into worshipping a golden calf). The common denominator in all these instances is simply that people take leave of the direction that they had been following previously. This accounts for the repeated use of "to the right or to the left" in connection with *sur*. In these cases, there is a straight path that should be followed; any wavering represents a failure of resolve to maintain the predetermined direction. Perhaps this is why this metaphor lends itself so nicely to issues of transgression, which is a deviation from the straight path. In the liturgy for Yom Kippur, we read, "We have turned aside from your good commandments and precepts, and it has not profited us." Sometimes, by contrast, the steady path that we are on is precisely the one that leads to repeated transgressions. And so the psalmist exhorts us simply to "turn away from evil and do good," just as we have previously deviated from the path of God's instructions.

It is striking throughout these passages that physical movement so readily lends itself to becoming a metaphor for moral (or immoral) behavior. Physical movement (at least purposeful movement) involves direction or orientation, intention and action. We are oriented toward some goal or destination, we form the intention to make progress toward that place, and then we physically move our bodies so as to accomplish the task. Similarly, moral behavior involves an orientation, an intention, and some concrete behavior. We identify the goal (of observing God's commandments), then we become motivated to pursue it, and finally we take the specific physical steps that enable us to progress toward it. Of course, the same is true for immoral behavior, as these biblical authors were keenly aware. And that is why physical movement is such a serviceable image for ethics—the very same steps are involved whether we set our sights on a desirable or an undesirable destination. Turning away—from evil toward good or the opposite—involves the same process. Pursuing good and pursuing evil are equally easy, it seems, for both involve precisely the same elements of choice.

But the metaphor that most fully captures the process of repentance is that of returning, most often expressed in the verb *shuv*. In its most basic sense, this designates the process of going back to our origins or returning to our proper, natural place. Powerful examples of this concept are found throughout the Bible.

> By the sweat of your brow
> Shall you get bread to eat,
> Until you return [*shuvkha*] to the ground—
> For from it you were taken.
> For dust you are,
> And to dust you shall return [*tashuv*].
>
> **(Genesis 3:19)**

> And the dust returns [*v'yasho*] to the ground
> As it was,
> And the lifebreath returns [*tashuv*] to God
> Who bestowed it.
>
> **(Ecclesiastes 12:7)**

This idea of something being restored to its primary or original location is frequently extended in the prophetic writings to the idea of the people of Israel being returned by God to their land. Their exile was a temporary (and perhaps necessary) consequence of their sinfulness, but their ultimate fate is to be returned to their native homeland (Jeremiah 12:15, 24:6–7, 31:1; Ezekiel 39:25).

It is but a small step from these—dust returning to its source and the Israelites to their land—to the notion of people returning to the ways of righteousness. "Turn back, O rebellious children / I will heal your afflictions!" (Jeremiah 3:22; also 3:14). And, in one of the prophet's more threatening moments, "I will bereave, I will destroy My people / For they would not turn back from their ways" (Jeremiah 15:7). In the passage that is read on the Shabbat before Yom Kippur, we find perhaps the most plaintive call for the Israelites to repent:

> Return, O Israel, to the LORD your God,
> For you have fallen because of your sin.
> Take words with you
> And return to the LORD.
>
> **(Hosea 14:2–3)**

In all these passages, the assumption appears to be that following God is a path to which we return, again and again, from the mistakes of waywardness and backsliding. The call is for the Israelites to find their way home in a moral and spiritual sense, just as they are to find their way home in the geographical sense.

Finally, some sources suggest that this return to God will be met with a parallel turning on God's part back toward us. In Jonah we read:

> Let everyone turn back from his evil ways and from the injustice of which he is guilty. Who knows but that God may turn and relent? He may turn back from His wrath, so that we do not perish.
>
> **(Jonah 3:8–9)**

The idea that God could also "turn" toward us in response to our turn to God should not surprise us. Indeed, it is merely the other half of the dynamic according to which God reacts with anger and judgment when we turn away from just behavior. As the prophets never tired of saying, God wants us to reform our ways:

> Is it my desire that a wicked man shall die?—says the Lord GOD. It is rather that he shall turn back from his ways and live.
>
> **(Ezekiel 18:23)**

> Seek the LORD while He can be found,
> Call to Him while He is near.
> Let the wicked give up his ways,
> The sinful man his plans;
> Let him turn back to the LORD,

And He will pardon him;
To our God,
For He freely forgives.

(Isaiah 55:6–7)

Returning in the moral as in the physical sense implies that there is, indeed, a way back. No matter how lost we are, finding our way home is possible. In fact, it is natural that we should return to a stable and intimate relationship with God, for this is just what God has hoped for.

All of us at one time or another have had the experience of losing our way. Sometimes, perhaps when we're traveling in a foreign place, we become completely disoriented. At first we think we know which way to head, but when we set out in that direction we discover that our own sense of direction has failed us. When we realize that we don't have the foggiest idea where we are or how to get to our destination, we are thoroughly lost. Such moments can arouse profound feelings of helplessness and even despair.

Being morally lost likewise involves a sense of despair. We have fallen into the same patterns of hurtful or self-destructive behavior so often we feel that we're beyond the point of being able to change. We don't know which direction to turn in order to find our way back to a life of honor and integrity. And before long we may come to believe that, for us at least, there is no way back. I have known many addicts who have lived for years with such feelings of helplessness.

Ultimately, though, the point of all these metaphors of movement is that the same steps that led us into the ditch of transgression can lead us back to the high road of ethical living. *Teshuvah*—returning—is the name Judaism gives to this process of retrieving our sense of direction. Repentance is the ultimate form of return. After turning our gaze away from God and straying from the straight path, we can still find our way back. And it is as simple as taking just one step in a new direction. For turning in a new direction, by as little as one degree, will lead us over time to a wholly different destination.

15

Step-by-Step on the Path of Repentance

Repentance must be preceded by the recognition of seven things: (1) the penitent must clearly recognize the heinousness of what he has done.... (2) He must be aware that his specific act was legally evil and ignominious.... (3) He must realize that retribution for his misdeed is inevitable.... (4) He must realize that his sin is noted and recorded in the book of his iniquities.... (5) He must be fully convinced that repentance is the remedy for his sickness and the road to recovery from his evil deed.... (6) He must conscientiously reflect upon the bounties the Creator had already bestowed upon him, and how he had rebelled against God instead of being grateful to Him.... (7) He must strenuously persevere in keeping away from the evil to which he had been addicted and firmly resolve in his heart and mind to renounce it.

Bachya ibn Pakuda, *Duties of the Heart* **7:3**

Throughout Jewish literature on *teshuvah* we find various attempts to delineate the steps involved in the process. Especially in the Middle Ages and early modern periods, pietistic writers seemed concerned to provide readers with moral handbooks, which were essentially *teshuvah* manuals. We might think of these as the precursors of the plethora of religiously inspired self-help books that are popular today. Although each author has his own scheme for analyzing the steps in the process of repentance, and some of these become quite elaborate, there are enough similarities among them that we can identify a common framework for the process of *teshuvah*. I would suggest that *teshuvah*, as it has traditionally been understood, comprises seven distinct steps: culpability, remorse, confession, apology, restitution, soul reckoning, and transformation. Each of these steps, of course, involves overcoming some resistance, clearing a hurdle, that would keep us from proceeding to the next stage in the process.

The very beginning of the process of doing *teshuvah* is to acknowledge, both to ourselves and to others, that we actually did the thing that was hurtful. This is often one of the hardest steps to take. Something in us resists the simple admission of guilt. Even as children, most of us experienced that primal impulse to evade responsibility. When an older adult confronted us about the lamp that was broken or the money that was missing, we may have tried to deny that we had any role in the unfortunate events. Someone else was to blame. We had nothing to do with it. At least, that's often our first line of self-defense. If we can dissociate ourselves from the act entirely, then we are free from all further need to deal with the consequences, in terms of either feeling guilty or being punished. Only when we squarely confront the fact that we did the deed in question can we move on to the other stages of *teshuvah*.

Most of us experience a tendency to deceive and evade responsibility, frequently in a subtler way than through sheer denial that we have any involvement whatsoever. Many times we are willing to acknowledge the fact that we did the deed in question (agency), but in the same breath deny that we are really at fault (culpability). Someone else made us do it, so we really have no liability for what we did. This game of "passing the buck" is widely practiced and familiar to all of us. The most notorious examples include war criminals who insist that they were "only following orders." Thus they can acknowledge that, yes, they did pull the trigger and murder scores of innocent people, but they are really not to blame, for they were just passive instruments of those who are truly at fault. Other, far more common examples of this sort of behavior show up regularly in news reports. People accused of some criminal wrongdoing protest that they are innocent. Their defense may be that their behavior falls within an exception to the law, or that they were unaware that what they did was illegal in the first place, or that the law itself is unjust. But whatever line of defense they choose, the bottom line remains the same: either I did not do the deed in question, or I did it, but I am not at fault. *Teshuvah* is only possible for those who can acknowledge both that they are guilty of some misdeed and that they alone are responsible for their moral failure.

The next stage in the process of repentance is more emotional than cognitive, for it involves our internal response to the truth of what we did. The penitent must reach a point of feeling remorse or regret for the mistakes of the past. We must come to believe that it would have been better not to have behaved in the way we did. The alternative, of course, is all too common. We regularly see people who are callous to the pain they have caused, who have essentially built a wall around their hearts, so that they can acknowledge in an abstract way that their deeds were wrong but cannot feel bad that they did them. This kind of attitude often shows up in the excuses people make for their behavior: "I know what I did was wrong, but others have done much worse. It's no big deal." Or, "So what if I made mistakes. I need to just close the door on the past and move on." But it is precisely the feeling of remorse that marks the turning point in the whole process of *teshuvah*. To feel regret about our actions is to begin to see ourselves as separable from our deeds. We now look back at what we have done from a moral vantage point that enables us to see that what we have done is wrong. We morally condemn those actions and so feel remorse that we did them in the first place. The feeling of remorse represents the reassertion of the moral self over the self who acted badly. No wonder, then, that judges often regard "lack of remorse" on the part of a convicted criminal as good reason to impose a heavier sentence. If we don't feel badly about what we have done, then we have removed ourselves twice from the moral sphere of society—first by our misconduct and then a second time by failing to exhibit the appropriate moral judgment about that very conduct.

From remorse to confession is a short step, from an internal judgment to an external expression. If we feel genuinely sorry about what we have done, then openly admitting our guilt is simply to say aloud what we have already said to ourselves. This is the first step in the process of doing *teshuvah* that involves bringing our mistake into the open. Exposing our moral failings to others, and especially to the very people we have wronged, is inherently risky. We may have to face the anger and disapproval of those we care about. We may face other sanctions—social ostracism or loss of status or other privileges—when we confess that we were wrong. At the very least, we make ourselves vulnerable by letting others know that we were in the wrong. And, of course, the more we stand to lose by openly acknowledging our errors, the more difficult it will be to do so.

From confession we move on to apology. Admitting that we failed is a prerequisite for apologizing, which almost always entails seeking forgiveness from the people we have harmed. The point of offering an apology is to repair a relationship that we have damaged through our behavior. Whether the apology succeeds in doing so will depend in large part on whether it is judged to be sincere and whether the injured party is prepared to forgive us. But whether successful or not, the goal is to demonstrate to others that we acknowledge the hurt we have caused and are openly sorry to have done so.[3] It is a plea to accept us as the remorseful person we are now, rather than to reject us as the hurtful person we were earlier. That is why apologies that are offered with conditional, equivocal words in them are rarely effective. "I am sorry if you took offense at what I did" is a long way from "I am sorry for offending you." It is only when we squarely accept responsibility for our own actions and express remorse for them that we have any reasonable expectation that others will find our apology meaningful.

Sometimes, however, words of apology alone are insufficient. If our offense was severe enough, and especially if it involved depriving others of material possessions, the victim is entitled to some kind of restitution. The offender needs to undo the wrong done to the extent possible—repairing or replacing what we have broken, returning what we have stolen, regaining the trust we have violated. Words of apology are a beginning, but only actions can demonstrate a real commitment to make right what we previously made wrong. And without demonstrating such a commitment, how sincere can our apology really be? Making the other person "whole" again is a way of actively reversing the effects of our misdeeds. We can never turn back the clock and literally undo our actions, but we can and must create a situation that is as close as possible to the state of affairs that would have been had we not behaved immorally. Anything less represents a failure to take full responsibility for the harm our actions caused others.

Having redressed our wrongs to the best of our ability, the next step in *teshuvah* is to turn inward to address the root of our harmful behavior. This involves a process of *cheshbon hanefesh*, or soul reckoning. What has caused us to be short-tempered with those we love? What character defect has led us to speak ill of others behind their backs? What makes us less generous than we know we should be? This is the point at which the focus of repentance shifts from the past to the future. For the goal is ultimately not only to take responsibility for what we have done but also to do better in the future. And that is surely impossible unless we have delved into the roots of our deeds, the experiences that have made us the sorts of people we are. Often this involves deep therapeutic work, as we explore relationships with parents or painful or even traumatic events that left their scars on our souls and now continue to affect us in ways that may be largely unconscious. As we bring these inner processes to consciousness, we become more self-aware and so gain the ability to make choices about how to live with these old wounds and psychic blind spots. Through *cheshbon hanefesh*, literally, "taking the measure of our souls," we have the opportunity to learn from the mistakes of the past and so, perhaps, to avoid repeating them. Needless to say, this sort of work continues throughout our lifetime as we come to understand more and more fully who we are as moral beings.

The process of *teshuvah* culminates in a moral transformation that encompasses both an inner reorientation and a change in outward behavior. The Talmud indicates that the ultimate test of whether or not we have done *teshuvah* is whether in the same circumstance we can resist the temptation to commit the same transgression. If we can, we have demonstrated that we are, indeed, different. Certain Sages suggest that the penitent is truly a new creation, in a significant way no longer the same person who was guilty of the wrongful actions. Some even suggest that the penitent should adopt a new name as a sign of this transformation. I once heard a person engaged in a profound process of repentance reflect on his past life, on times when he had abused drugs and alcohol. He commented that "the person who did those things was me, but I am no longer that person." This captures precisely the mystery and wonder of *teshuvah*, for the moral transformation that occurs in the penitent is tantamount to becoming, if not literally a different person, a radically different sort of person. And that means a person who could not, or would not, fall into the same patterns of harmful behavior again.

Of course, the path of repentance is not short or straight. It often doubles back on itself, and it would be a mistake to assume that the steps outlined here are always followed in rigid, chronological order. The point, rather, is to notice that the process is multifaceted and encompasses many different kinds of steps—some backward-looking and others forward-looking, some focused on attitudes and others on behaviors. All together they constitute a journey that all of us can recognize and join.

16

It Is I

One of the foundations of penitence, in human
thought, is a person's recognition of responsibility
for his actions, which derives from a belief in
man's free will. This is also the substance of the
confession that is part of the commandment of
penitence, in which the person acknowledges that
no other cause is to be blamed for his misdeed
and its consequences but he himself.

Rabbi Abraham Isaac Kook[4]

Accepting responsibility is the very first step in the process of
doing *teshuvah*. It is also one of the most difficult. What is it
about acknowledging that we are at fault that sends us running
for cover, looking for excuses, casting blame on others, and
engaging in sometimes elaborate strategies of denial?

I know from my own experience just how difficult it is to
"own" my own mistakes. Small mistakes—failing to do something
I had promised, or breaking something that I had been entrusted
with—needed to be covered up. After all, as the favorite child in
my family, I had been told since early childhood that I was a
"model child." In my parents' eyes, I could do no wrong. Over
time I came to feel profoundly ashamed if I failed to live up to
those (perhaps unrealistically high) expectations. Partly, I didn't
want to disappoint my parents, I suppose, but more important, I
didn't want to deal with the disillusionment that would follow if I
had to confront the fact that I wasn't as perfect as I expected myself
to be. So, I became a perfectionist and a pleaser, committed to

doing everything in my power to fixing whatever mistakes I made before they (and I) could be discovered.

In raising my own children, I told them repeatedly that I might not always approve of everything they did, but I would always love them just the same, no matter what. I would like to believe that, in parenting them this way, I have helped them grow to adulthood without the need to obsessively cover up any mistakes they make. But, on reflection, even this message does not really address the issue. For it is ultimately artificial to separate "what we do" from "who we are"; after all, we *are* the people who are capable of *doing* all sorts of wrongs, large and small. The real problem is that we cannot admit to ourselves or others who we are.

We are, all of us, flawed. And virtually all of us are ashamed to admit that. To be sure, we can "admit" it in a verbal, matter-of-fact sort of way. But we don't wish to genuinely confront our failings, because we don't want to acknowledge what they say about *us*. We are less than we wish we were, less than others expect us to be, less than we pretend to be. And, for most of us, that is unacceptable, if not completely intolerable.

The only antidote to this failure of moral courage is to adopt the view that we are acceptable, even lovable, as the imperfect people we are. Our moral shortcomings do not need to be hidden or segregated so that we can retain an imaginary sense of moral acceptability. We are not "less" because of our misdeeds; however, we do impoverish ourselves spiritually and morally when we fail to accept ourselves, faults and all.

That simple act of accepting ourselves enables us to accept responsibility for the times we slighted a friend, took something we weren't entitled to, or responded harshly to a co-worker when we should have been kinder. When we accept ourselves in this way, we do not have to hide from ourselves or others. We are free to take responsibility for *all* of what we do. Therein lies the great paradox: in the effort to be free of wrongdoing, we make ourselves slaves to an image of perfection that is unattainable. But accepting responsibility for our mistakes brings us a new kind of freedom, the freedom to be fully ourselves with one another and before God. Freeing ourselves in this way is the very first step on the path of *teshuvah*.

17

Remorse

"Verily God loves those who turn unto Him [in repentance], and He loves those who purify themselves" (Qur'an 2:222). It was asked, "O Messenger of God, what is the sign of repentance?" He replied, "Remorse."

'Abd al-Karim al-Qushayri[5]

Remorse is at the very heart of repentance. To feel remorse is more than just "being sorry" for what we have done. It signals a new perspective on our deeds in the past, on ourselves in the present, and on our plans for the future. It is the quintessential sign of repentance, as the Sufi al-Qushayri recognized, because it reflects a (paradoxical) double movement of the self, both owning our past and distancing ourselves from it.

Remorse grows from a profound awareness of my moral failings. Looking back, I see clearly what I have heretofore failed to see—perhaps unwittingly, perhaps willfully—namely, that I have harmed others by my actions. But it is not just to note in a detached way that the things I did had negative effects on others. It is to take responsibility for them, to accept that (whatever I may have claimed to the contrary notwithstanding) the fault lies with *me*—not with circumstances beyond my control. And it is to regret those actions, in a way that many of us fail to do when we resort to the myriad excuses that might justify our hurtful actions: that "they deserved it," that "I couldn't help myself," that "anyone in my circumstances would have done the same thing," and so forth. All these, and similar

85

rationalizations, are meant to excuse ourselves and so avoid culpability.

But remorse is precisely the opposite of such avoidance. It is a wholehearted embrace of culpability. To feel remorse is to accept responsibility for our actions, to know deeply that those actions reflect on our moral character and to be willing to face the consequences of that responsibility. In that sense, remorse is the quintessential sign of the morally responsible self. When people express remorse—even if they have committed heinous crimes—we tend to view them with some sympathy. Why? Because the expression of remorse, if it is genuine, indicates that the individuals before us have taken responsibility for their misdeeds. And that, by itself, shows that they have regained a sense of moral judgment. Such judgment may not mitigate the wrongs they have done, but it surely casts them in a different light.

Remorse is the fruit of some prior process of moral self-reflection in terms of which the offender now judges her former deeds as condemnable. And this is where the second movement referred to above comes into play. For at the same time that remorse represents an embrace of the past, it also represents a break from it. The offender now stands apart from past behavior and in judgment of it. To be remorseful is simultaneously to face squarely the severity of our failings and to stand apart from them, judging them from the standpoint of a higher moral plane. This is precisely why it represents the essence of the inner moral transformation that we call repentance: we own our past and also disown it.

Remorse, then, is closely linked with a kind of resolve. When we truly feel remorseful, we cannot help but wish not to repeat what we have done; the very willingness to consider repeating the offense is proof positive that we don't genuinely regret the transgression. This may be why Maimonides, in his definition of repentance, links remorse with the resolve not to sin again:

> What is *teshuvah*? It is when a sinner abandons his sin and removes it from his thoughts, and resolves in his heart not to do that deed again. As it says, "Let the wicked man forsake his way, and the unrighteous man his thoughts" (Isaiah 55:7). And so he repents for the past. As it says, "After I had turned

away, I repented" (Jeremiah 31:18). And he will call the
Knower of Secrets to testify against him that he will never
again return to this sin. As it says, "Nor shall we say ever
again to the work of our hands, 'You are our God'" (Hosea
14:4). And he must confess in words these things that he has
resolved in his heart.

(*Mishneh Torah*, **Laws of Repentance 2:2**)

Remorse and the explicit determination not to fall into the same
transgression again are the essence of repentance. Without this
step, taking responsibility, providing restitution, and even seeking
forgiveness are all empty gestures.

Remorse is thus the pivotal point on the path of repentance.
To feel remorse is already to have demonstrated that a certain
moral rehabilitation has taken place within, that conscience, or the
willingness to listen to it, has reasserted itself. No wonder that one
of the harshest condemnations we have of a hardened criminal is
that "he showed no remorse." Lack of remorse is a second moral
failing, which intensifies and exacerbates the original offense.
When a person shows no remorse, he implicitly (and in some cases
explicitly) condones his transgressions, regards them as morally
unobjectionable, and (in truly egregious cases) even morally praise-
worthy. The famous example of Adolf Eichmann, who supposedly
felt that he could "leap into his grave laughing" at the thought of
the six million Jews whose annihilation he masterminded, is chill-
ing beyond words. By contrast, in many cases a jury or judge will
impose a lighter sentence on a criminal who does show remorse.
It is a sign of moral transformation and so changes our assessment
of the criminal's guilt. It is as though the criminal's own self-
condemnation opens the door for us to soften ours.

But remorse is also about the future. For it is impossible to
feel genuinely remorseful and at the same time wish to continue
misbehaving in the same ways. Remorse arises exactly at the
juncture between looking back at our past with dismay and looking toward a new life that is still more removed from those misdeeds. It is the fruit of a process of moral transformation already
begun, as well as the root of a new moral life that needs to be built
on the ruins of the old one. The way forward may not yet be clear

for the offender, but the feeling of remorse signals that some sort of change is called for. It is not possible to continue as in the past. And so remorse propels the offender forward, in search of a way to start anew. In this sense, though remorse is not a pleasant experience, it is invariably a growthful one, and this may lead the penitent to feel a sense of gratitude at the feeling of remorse. It signals that the process of moral rehabilitation is already under way. Regret over the past, then, presupposes that the self has risen to a new, higher level and also is the process through which this higher self emerges and establishes itself.[6]

In the end, then, remorse can be the beginning of a kind of hope that is one of the hallmarks of repentance. The other stages of repentance—apology, restitution, and the work of self-transformation—can only unfold where remorse has prepared the way. In the words of Harold O. J. Brown, one Christian writer:

> Repentance implies restitution and restoration, and thus implies a future that is not bound by the habits and vices of the past.... Repentance follows upon sorrow about the past, but sorrow of a particular kind; hopeful sorrow, if we may put it thus.[7]

In precisely this way, remorse is the crux of the inner process of repentance. It looks both backward and forward; it presupposes a willingness to assume moral responsibility and points to the need for further moral transformation; it couples sadness with hopefulness. If repentance is "turning," then remorse is the pivot of that turn, for it is the emotion that we inevitably feel when we stand poised between the awareness of our past transgressions and the resolve to do something about them.

18

Announce Your Sins

Just as the sacrifice is burnt upon the altar so do
we burn down, by our act of confession, our well-
barricaded complacency, our overblown pride,
our artificial existence.
Rabbi Joseph B. Soloveitchik[8]

Most of the time when we do something we know to be
wrong, we try to hide it. The impulse is nearly immediate
and frequently irresistible. We feel guilty that we cheated on our
taxes, so when we are audited, we insist it was an innocent mistake. We are ashamed that we were stopped for drunk driving, so
when we are questioned about it, we sweep it under the rug. In
this way, we hope to protect our reputations in the eyes of others.
Sometimes we even imagine that if we can just dissociate ourselves from our own objectionable behavior, we can live with ourselves in peace. It is a natural impulse, and it never works.

Everyone who writes about the process of *teshuvah* identifies
confession as a key element in the process. We need to admit our
wrongs—clearly, forthrightly, and publicly. These days the idea of
standing up in a public setting and announcing our transgressions
strikes us as extreme, perhaps even bizarre, behavior. Most of us
would be mortified at the very thought of baring our souls in public (though, interestingly, it happens quite routinely on daytime
TV talk shows). But the Rabbis who promoted this understood
something that we have forgotten: that the antidote to shame is
disclosure. Feelings of shame thrive in secrecy; they evaporate in
the bright light of day.

Here is how Maimonides describes the requirement of confession:

> It is very praiseworthy for the penitent to confess publicly and announce his sins, and reveal to others the transgressions he committed against his fellow. He should say to them, "Truly I have sinned against so-and-so by doing such-and-such. But now I am turning and repenting." Everyone who is arrogant and doesn't reveal but rather conceals his sins—his *teshuvah* isn't complete. As it says, "One who conceals his transgressions does not succeed" (Proverbs 28:13).
>
> (*Mishneh Torah*, **Laws of Repentance 2:5**)

What good could possibly come from such public confessionals? Surely it would be better to admit our failings in a very private setting, if we chose to reveal them at all.

To confess our failings in public is to allow ourselves to be seen, warts and all. We drop the pretense of being better than we really are and allow ourselves to appear in public just as we are in private. By casting off the public persona and overcoming the resistance we generally feel to sharing our shortcomings, we free ourselves from the need to continually polish our facade of rectitude. Because, though we may not always realize it, we expend a good deal of effort day after day in pretending to be purer than we really are. I know from my own experience that it is hard work to hide the little failings that mar our self-image. Once we drop that facade, we can channel all that energy into addressing our shortcomings, rather than hiding them.

Confession, then, brings a kind of wholeness. It enables us to quit compartmentalizing ourselves into "public" and "private," "upstanding citizen" and "moral failure." It involves, as a therapist once put it to me, living transparently. It is an announcement not that I am proud of my transgressions, but that I am a person with flaws, exactly like everyone else. This kind of pronouncement is both liberating and cathartic, as well as connecting. Because anyone listening will surely discover that she, too, shares these flaws, or others no less serious. Confession is a step in the process of reclaiming our humanity, neither boasting of our misdeeds nor being ashamed of them.

Anyone who, like me, has spent time in a twelve-step recovery program knows the power of such public confessions. When one member of the group reveals the ways in which addiction has caused him to do shameful things, details the ways in which he has disappointed himself and others, and explains the lengths to which he went to cover his tracks, the experience is transformative. The speaker feels unburdened, while those listening feel privileged to have sat in the presence of a person engaged in real *teshuvah*. Such moments are sacred, precisely because when we reveal our deepest secrets, and when we listen to others doing the same, we have a powerful sense of sharing our common humanity. I strongly suspect that this experience explains in large measure why twelve-step groups of all kinds have proliferated throughout the world. We all need a safe place where we can engage in public confession.

To be sure, such confessions presume a very high degree of trust and confidentiality. It would be foolhardy, to say nothing of impractical and counterproductive, to confess our sins to random strangers passing on the street. But in the context of a close-knit circle of fellow penitents, the regular practice of confession breaks down our innate resistance to self-disclosure. And it is only when we see ourselves—and allow others to see us—as we really are that we can reach a level of self-acceptance that is the very prerequisite for the self-transformation we call *teshuvah*.

19

Apologize Yet Again

Apology is an act that would not be required if
the wrong had not been done, and it is an act
that is specifically and explicitly directed to the
wronged party. It is, furthermore, an act that
obviously *gives something* to the wronged party.
Apology constitutes an overt disavowal of the past
wrong act, and (more importantly) openly gives
an explicit assurance of future good intention.

Richard Cross[9]

Most of us have trouble apologizing to those we have hurt.
We may wish to conceal the very fact that we are responsible for our moral shortcomings. We may fear that there will be recriminations, or that others will love us less, or that we will lose our position if our misconduct comes into the open. Even when we feel genuinely remorseful for what we have done—perhaps especially then—we would rather not confront those we have harmed and so lower ourselves in our own eyes and theirs.

No wonder, then, that so many apologies are flawed. They come too late, long after our words might have made a difference to the other. Or they come couched in equivocal language ("I'm sorry if you were offended by what I said"), which subtly shifts responsibility from what I said to how the other person heard it. Or we say the right words, but without the tone of genuine remorse in our voice that alone communicates sincerity.

Given the inherent difficulties of apologizing, it is striking that Jewish tradition demands that we apologize not only once, but multiple times when we have offended another person. Here is how Maimonides summarizes the law:

> Even if one only injured the other in words [and not in deeds], he must pacify him and approach him until he forgives him. If his fellow does not wish to forgive him, the other person brings a line of three of his friends who [in turn] approach the offended person and request from him [that he grant forgiveness]. If he is not accepting of them, he brings a second [cadre of friends] and then a third. If he still does not wish [to grant forgiveness], one leaves him and goes his own way, and the person who would not forgive is himself the sinner.
>
> (*Mishneh Torah,* **Laws of Repentance 2:9–10**)

The demand that we make several efforts to apologize, even enlisting friends to attest to our sincerity, reflects a recognition that this is difficult to do well. All the more reason why a single gesture of apology is inadequate. The onus is on the offender to demonstrate that she is truly sorry, and the very lengths she is required to go to in that effort may testify to her intention.

Obtaining forgiveness from the offended party is essential to the offender's process of *teshuvah.* Judaism teaches that the offenses we commit against others cannot be forgiven by God on Yom Kippur *unless* those we have harmed forgive us first. So the offender must continue to apologize and ask for forgiveness in order to fully repent.

The conclusion of this passage points to a limiting condition. The offender is not required to continue apologizing forever. What is required is that he make a good faith effort—a considerable effort, at that—to obtain forgiveness. Three attempts, it seems, is prima facie evidence of his sincerity. After that, he is relieved of his responsibility. The offender's process of *teshuvah* need not be held captive to a person too hardhearted or resentful to forgive.

In our time, we have unfortunately lost much of this commitment to apologize wholeheartedly and repeatedly. But those of us who have worked hard to regain the trust of others know that a single effort is never sufficient. The work of repairing a broken relationship needs to be commensurate with the pain that our actions caused. If the harm involved is significant, there is no quick and easy way to undo it. Forgiveness is not free or, in many cases, even cheap—nor should it be. The effort involved in apologizing again and again demonstrates that we are engaged in a genuine process of *teshuvah*, and seeing this is precisely what enables the injured party to forgive and reenter the relationship.

The need for sincere apology is an integral component in genuine *teshuvah*. No wonder, then, that the tradition places such an emphasis on the importance of this step, difficult as it is. When we return again and again to express our remorse and attempt to make peace with our neighbors, we gain a healthy respect for the power of our misdeeds and the difficulty of compensating for them. And that awareness, once acquired, serves both to deter us from further transgressions and to prompt us to deeper levels of self-examination.

20

Making Others Whole Again

For transgressions between one person and another,
such as injury, cursing, stealing, and similar offenses,
a person is never forgiven until he gives the other
what is owed to him, and pacifies him.

Maimonides, *Mishneh Torah*, Laws of Repentance 2:9

There is no *teshuvah* that does not reverse the real harm our actions have caused. Confession and apology are important, and in cases where the harm was strictly emotional, they may go a long way toward repairing the damage our words have caused. But when we cause others physical suffering or monetary loss, there is no way to restore our moral standing without returning whatever we have taken. Remorse is no substitute for restitution.

To harm another is to incur a moral debt. Whether we take someone's property or their dignity, we owe them something. And that debt can only be repaid in the same currency in which it was incurred—a financial loss requires a monetary response, an insult or some other slight requires that we verbally repair the harm to the relationship involved. Sometimes, too, what is called for is more than a simple quid pro quo. If I have cheated a business partner, I need both to repay the money I wrongly took and also to repair the breach of trust my actions caused. Doing the latter will almost certainly be far harder, and take far longer, than the financial restitution. It will require a series of actions, both substantive and symbolic, that demonstrate commitment, integrity, and genuine concern. All this is part of making the other whole or, in Maimonides' words, "pacifying our fellow."

95

As obvious as this seems, it is remarkable how frequently it is overlooked or minimized. Some would have us believe that sins are primarily offenses against God and so we can set things right by confessing our sins to God and engaging in rituals of penance. Others emphasize that the problem is primarily internal to the sinner, who must engage in soul searching and recommit to a path of righteousness. And there is truth in both these perspectives. But Judaism has always been clear that sin is first and foremost a *moral* problem, that is, a problem between one person and another. Repentance, then, is possible only on the plane of interpersonal relations, through concrete deeds that "right the scales" between the people involved.

Sometimes righting the scales is possible even though direct restitution to our victims is not. In the film *Gandhi*, there is one scene that has always captured for me the essence of restitution. In the midst of one of his famous hunger strikes, Gandhi is approached by a Hindu fighter who acknowledges that he has just killed several Muslims during one of the battles that raged in that period. The fighter is looking for Gandhi to forgive him, but instead he simply looks back at the Hindu and tells him he must go out and find a Muslim orphan, whose parents have been killed in the violence, adopt that child, and raise him as a Muslim in his own home. The Hindu fighter is plainly horrified, but also awed, by Gandhi's suggestion, for he realizes immediately both how terribly difficult this is, and also how essential it is to achieving the forgiveness he seeks. Gandhi understood that it is not always possible to provide perfect restitution to our victims, but this does not preclude the possibility of taking steps to "right the scales" by doing the kind of deed that counteracts the wrong we have done.

There are no shortcuts on the path of repentance. We cannot find wholeness ourselves if we do not guarantee it to those we have harmed. And that harm is not in our souls or in our relationships to God—or not only there—but right here in the social world where we interact with one another. When we insist on restitution, we are affirming that the keys to repentance are held by the very people we have hurt.

21

Soul Reckoning

When Sahl ibn 'Abdullah was asked about repentance, he responded, "It is to never forget your
fault." When Junayd was asked about repentance,
he said, "It is forgetting your fault."

Abu Nasr as-Sarraj[10]

Cheshbon hanefesh, literally a "reckoning [or accounting] of the
soul" is more than some simple enumeration of our failings and
merits on a spreadsheet, though the metaphor of the balance sheet
is instructive in certain respects. Soul reckoning involves self-
knowledge, the ability to recognize and counter our own propen-
sity to self-deception, in other words, rigorous honesty. It is a
coming to terms not only with the deeds we have done but also
with the persons we have become. Without engaging in such a
process—indeed, without cultivating a deeper and deeper capacity
for this sort of self-reflection—the way of repentance is closed to us.

It is a given among those who have written about repentance
that the human capacity for self-deception is virtually endless. We
know only too well how readily we can hide from ourselves,
turning our gaze away from those faults and character flaws that,
if confronted openly, would challenge our perception of ourselves
as upright. We are often invested in that sense of our own blame-
lessness and in preserving that image of ourselves in the eyes of
others. Lying to ourselves and to others comes naturally to most
of us. It is a well-trodden path and frequently a deeply entrenched
habit. Soul reckoning calls us to break free from that habit and
embark on a very different path.

Soul reckoning requires us to look squarely at our own fallibility, to take stock of exactly where we have fallen short of the
moral behavior that is expected of us (and that we expect of ourselves). The result of shining the light of self-scrutiny on ourselves
can be unnerving, even shattering. The way we treated our parents or our children was just plain unacceptable; our failure to
respond to the needs of others was inexcusable. The stories that
we have told ourselves to justify, avoid, and/or minimize our
shortcomings are challenged and have to be rewritten or even
rejected. At stake is nothing less than our sense of self. If we look
at ourselves honestly, the picture is likely to be less flattering than
we would like. After all, this is exactly why we have avoided such
moral self-assessment in the first place. But once we overcome
that innate inner resistance, we face the challenge of what to do
with our newfound awareness of our own moral failings. How
shall we live with ourselves, if this is who we really are?

For many, especially those who may suffer from low self-
esteem for other reasons, soul reckoning of this sort can trigger a
downward spiral of self-rejection, self-flagellation, or even self-
hatred. Self-condemnation is always painful and may even be
self-destructive. But genuine soul reckoning is meant to lead us
down a different path, toward acceptance and integration. How
does this happen?

Seeing our own failings more clearly can and should be an
impetus to deeper moral sensitivity and moral growth. It is the
spur to repentance, showing us where we have work to do and so
enabling us to make progress, by addressing those shortcomings,
holding ourselves accountable, repairing our relationships with
others, and taking all the other steps in the process of repentance
that are explored throughout this book.

I once engaged in a couple of small ethnographic studies of
the ethics of professionals—one focused on several physicians, the
other on trial court judges. Both groups of professionals confided
that they often struggle with their own moral mistakes—doctors
who miss a diagnosis, judges who allow their personal biases to
affect their rulings. In the case of physicians, especially, such mistakes can be extremely harmful, even fatal. All the professionals I
spoke with acknowledged making such mistakes, and not only in

the early stages of their careers. Indeed, it was striking that many talked about cultivating a sense of their own fallibility, focusing on those mistakes, as a way of holding themselves accountable to the highest ethical standards of their professions. In the same way all of us can look at our mistakes honestly and examine them carefully, not to reinforce a sense of failure or moral turpitude, but just the opposite—to motivate ourselves to reach higher and make better choices in the future.[11]

For this is the paradox of soul reckoning. It is a kind of dwelling on our shortcomings for the purpose of undoing them, looking to the past in order to create a different future. "The unexamined life is not worth living," said Socrates. Penitents would agree, adding that it is precisely by examining our lives, especially our flaws, that we can set ourselves on the path of moral improvement. This is not self-knowledge for its own sake, and certainly not a prescription for wallowing in self-pity or an excuse for self-recrimination. Soul reckoning is a tool for moral regeneration. The transgressions of the past need to be scrutinized so that they can be overcome, set aside, and ultimately redeemed.

The challenge of engaging in soul reckoning, then, is to claim the past and also disclaim it. Rabbi Joseph B. Soloveitchik, one of the preeminent Orthodox thinkers of the twentieth century, captured this problem when he wrote about the penitent:

> He returns to his starting point, to where he stood prior to embarking upon the road of sin, and everything that has occurred in the meantime disappears, as if it had never been.... This repentance does not entail making a clean break with the past or obliterating memories. It allows man, at one and the same time, to continue to identify with the past and still to return to God in repentance.[12]

It is in this sense that we must understand the seemingly contradictory answers that the two Muslim thinkers quoted in the opening epigraph give to the question of what repentance requires. Sahl ibn 'Abdullah recognizes that soul reckoning is all about remembering our faults and never turning our gaze away from them. For the danger is that as soon as we suspend this rigorous self-examination, we will lose opportunities for self-knowledge and the potential to become better selves. Junayd, by contrast, recognizes that if we dwell on our failings, we will lose our faith in the possibility of changing ourselves. The goal is to turn away from our transgressions completely, leave them entirely behind us, so that we can create a new moral self.

The process of soul reckoning encompasses both truths—we must never turn away from the awareness of our faults precisely so that we can turn away from them. The goal is a kind of remembering that leads to forgetting. For penitents know that it is when we hide our faults from ourselves that they retain their hold over us, but by examining them thoroughly, we assert our freedom from them.

22

Teshuvah, Complete and Unending

> What is complete *teshuvah*? When one comes upon
> a situation in which he once transgressed, and it is
> possible to do so again, but he refrains and doesn't
> transgress on account of his repentance.
>
> **Maimonides,** *Mishneh Torah,* **Laws of Repentance 2:1**

How do we know when we have really done *teshuvah*? Are we
done when we feel sufficiently remorseful? When we have
repaired the relationships that we have broken? When others forgive us for our hurtful behavior? How much *teshuvah* is enough?

The Rabbis were clear that *teshuvah,* as a process of personal
transformation, is only complete when a person's behavior has
definitively changed. A change of heart is essential to the process,
but it is purely internal and subjective. Making restitution and
seeking and obtaining forgiveness from others are all crucial, but
they only address past wrongs. The real test comes in the penitent's behavior going forward.

There is a simple logic to this. The transgressions we committed in the past were tangible, hurtful deeds. So, too, the *teshuvah* we seek must express itself in contrary deeds. If our outward
behavior hasn't changed, then surely whatever changes have
taken place within have not yet expressed themselves in the only
way that really counts, which is in the way we treat others. We
may have traveled a long way on the path of repentance, but our
teshuvah is not yet complete. The inner transformation brought

about by earlier steps in the process must be realized in real, concrete behavioral changes.

On the one hand, this behavioral criterion for successful *teshuvah* probably reflects the Rabbis' preoccupation with law and with the sorts of observable deeds that law can attempt to regulate. But it may also reveal a deeper conviction—that *teshuvah* aims to make us into substantially different people than we were in the past. And we can only be sure that we really are different when we carry ourselves differently in the world. This may account for the fact that the Rabbis specify that we must be faced with the same situation in which we once transgressed and demonstrate that we are capable of making a different choice. In the Talmud, Rabbi Judah provides a pointed gloss: "with the same woman, at the same time, in the same place." Only when the circumstances are precisely repeated can we fully demonstrate that we can and will resist the very same temptations to which we succumbed in the past. Then we can be sure that our *teshuvah* is complete.

When we can be really different in the future than we were in the past, then we have truly disavowed our transgressions. Among the addicts whose stories I have heard are those who have a long history of seeing prostitutes or engaging in phone sex. They often struggle to break free from these habitual behaviors and resolve to change, but many times these resolutions are broken. But when they find themselves back in a situation where they once transgressed and definitively break from the past, they discover a new sense of self-esteem. They really have become different people who have learned from the past and are determined not to repeat it. And that is when genuine healing begins.

The irony, though, is that by this standard "complete *teshuvah*" is never complete. Each situation in life presents penitents with a new challenge: can we resist the impulse to misbehave *this* time? Even if we have succeeded in breaking the pattern many times before, there are no guarantees. We just might fall back into an old, hurtful behavior, because the work of moral transformation is not just arduous, it is never perfect. Flawed creatures that we are, we continually struggle with our *yetzer ha-ra*.

No matter how much soul reckoning we have done, no matter how well trod the path of repentance may be, we may yet lose our way.

The task is infinite. The work of *teshuvah* is never done.

Part IV

Teshuvah in Three
Dimensions

23

Repentance, Prayer, and Righteousness

But repentance, prayer, and righteousness
avert the severity of the [divine] decree.
Traditional High Holy Day prayer book

Teshuvah can be understood properly only when we appreciate its many dimensions and the ways in which they intersect. These dimensions have been identified in different ways, and perhaps no single set of categories is quite adequate to capture the subtleties of everything the Jewish tradition has said about *teshuvah*. But at the outset it is helpful to think about *teshuvah* as a psychological, moral, and spiritual concept. In some of these reflections, a single dimension of *teshuvah* comes into focus; in others, we see the intersection of two or all three of these dimensions. Indeed, much of what Judaism has to say about *teshuvah* can be organized around the ways in which various thinkers across the centuries have understood the interrelationships among its psychological, moral, and spiritual dimensions.

On the psychological level, *teshuvah* is about the inner life. Here the key questions are: Who am I really? How do I understand my own "evil inclination" and its relationship to my "good inclination"? How can I turn myself, literally reorient my life, so as to maximize my own potential for goodness? Answering these questions is the work of *cheshbon hanefesh*, which I have translated literally as "soul reckoning." It involves what the twelve steps of Alcoholics Anonymous (AA) refer to as "taking a searching and fearless moral inventory of ourselves." For many, this entails profound thera-peutic work with the help of a professional psychologist or psychi-atrist. As we peel away the layers of our psyches, we discover where we harbor pain and distrust, which sorts of experiences tend to trigger strong reactions, which sorts of people we are drawn to and repelled by, the ways in which our own personali-ties have been shaped by many forces and experiences over many years, and so on. Taken together, these insights help us see where our own blind spots are and how to minimize the likelihood that they will hamper our ability to behave morally. Needless to say, this work can be extremely difficult and can stretch over many years until we reach a point where we can say we truly know our-selves. Let us call this work of reorientation and moral self-explo-ration "repentance" in the narrowest sense.[1]

On the spiritual level, *teshuvah* is about restoring a broken relationship with God. Judaism teaches us that all our transgres-sions against one another are also violations of our obligations to God. This is one of the most profound insights that Judaism offers us about the moral life, namely, that it is a life lived before God and in relation to God. However we understand God—and we certainly don't need to imagine God in the anthropomorphic terms that many biblical texts and prayers use—we know that we are accountable for the choices we make before the Source of life, goodness, and truth. So when we fail our family members, our friends and co-workers, our community, we also fail God and need to reestablish a connection to the Divine. We have strayed and we are asked to turn again toward God, and to place a rela-tionship to goodness and truth—which are the hallmarks of the Divine—at the center of our lives once again. This takes us beyond the inner work of repentance into the realm of supplica-tion. For in our heart of hearts we know that we do not do this work alone. Rather, it involves opening ourselves up to the help that comes from outside us. Traditionally, this sort of spiritual reconnection occurs in the context of worship, so let's call this aspect of the process of turning "prayer."

On the moral level, *teshuvah* is about restoring our relation-ships to those we have hurt, to the best of our ability. This is the part of the process that most of us immediately associate with *teshuvah*—offering our sincere apologies, asking for forgiveness, and, where possible, making restitution. These gestures all involve giving something to the person or people we have offended. For whether the harm involved was emotional (a harsh word, a failure to show appropriate concern or to acknowledge some other wrong we committed in the past) or material (something we stole, some physical damage we caused), our actions have deprived others of something that was theirs. We right the wrong we have done by giving back what we have taken away, sometimes by words that express our concern to counteract our prior lack of concern, sometimes by material possessions that replace those that we took or ruined. In all of these cases, the moral requirement is that we make those we have hurt "whole" by righting the scales again, restoring what we have wrongfully taken. This social aspect of *teshuvah* is, perhaps, the hardest part of all. It requires us to face those we have hurt and, in facing them, to humble ourselves through frank admission of wrongdoing, offering amends, and restoring what we have taken. Let us call this moral dimension of the process "righteousness."

Teshuvah operates at all these levels, and Jewish tradition insists that we cannot sidestep any of them. There are no shortcuts. We cannot do the necessary inner work of self-evaluation and overlook the restitution to our neighbors. Similarly, we cannot reconnect with God and then suppose that we are free to ignore the challenges of taking our moral inventory. To truly "turn" we must restore our broken relationships on all levels—with ourselves, with God, and with others.

This is what *teshuvah* involves; nothing less will suffice. It is arduous work, for it is nothing else than the work of building moral character, creating spiritual connection, and restoring interpersonal relationships, day after day, continuously. It is also enormously powerful work, capable of changing the course of our lives and even of our standing with God. That is why one of the high points of the traditional High Holy Day liturgy occurs when we imagine God judging each of us individually, determining our destiny in the coming year—who shall live and who shall die—and tremble with the realization that our fate hangs in the balance.

24

Being Fully Oneself

[Man's] conscience is the voice which calls him back to
himself, it permits him to know what he ought to do in
order to become himself, it helps him to remain aware
of the aims of his life and of the norms necessary for
the attainment of these aims.

Erich Fromm[2]

Who are we? How shall we understand what is at the very
core of our lives, those elements that define our humanity?
And what role does the process of sinning and repenting play in
our development as people? These questions have been pondered
by religious thinkers for centuries and, more recently, by psychologists interested in exploring the depths of our self-awareness and
the processes of our self-realization. Beneath any theory of human
development lies a set of assumptions about human nature and
what is required for human flourishing. How have modern psychologists understood moral development, and how are these
views related to *teshuvah*, as we understand it?

In the work of "humanistic psychologists"—thinkers including Rollo May, Abraham Maslow, Carl Rogers, and Erich Fromm,
among others—we find a number of common themes. These
thinkers all believed that humans have an innate need for self-
realization and that the process of "becoming a person," to borrow
Rogers's phrase, involves seeking integration, wholeness, and
meaning in life. This process is taken to be natural, and the role
of the therapist is merely to facilitate the individual's movement
toward self-actualization. In Maslow's words:

> Man demonstrates *in his own nature* a pressure toward fuller and fuller being, more and more perfect actualization of his humanness in exactly the same naturalistic, scientific sense that an acorn may be said to be "pressing toward" being an oak tree, or that a tiger can be observed to "push toward" being tigerish, or a horse toward being equine.... The environment does not give him potentialities and capacities; he *has* them in inchoate or embryonic form, just exactly as he has embryonic arms and legs. And creativeness, spontaneity, selfhood, authenticity, caring for others, being able to love, yearning for truth are embryonic potentialities belong to his species-membership just as much as are his arms and legs and brain and eyes.[3]

This is a fundamentally positive view of humankind, one that takes for granted that human beings are essentially "hardwired" to seek authenticity and wholeness. Circumstances of all sorts—painful personal experiences, social pressures, institutional expectations—conspire to constrain us and inhibit us from reaching this goal. But we all have the capacity to live meaningful lives as creative, responsible people.

Of course, all these thinkers recognized that the road to living such a meaningful life can be long and arduous. In Rollo May's words, "Freedom does not come automatically; it is achieved. And it is not gained at a single bound; it must be achieved every day."[4] For May and others, this freedom requires that people assume moral responsibility for their own lives and those around them. This entails taking responsibility for the degree of happiness and fulfillment we find in life, as well as the extent to which we actualize our potential for creativity, goodness, and integration. We are the masters of our souls, and our task in life—no matter what our cultural or religious or socioeconomic background—is the same: to become fully who we are.

This way of viewing human personhood is strikingly consonant with the goals of *teshuvah*. In the process of soul reckoning, we achieve greater self-knowledge and so, too, greater freedom. For only when we truly know ourselves can we break the invisible chains that keep us enslaved to old patterns of behavior.

There is much in life that obscures the truth of our existence and so causes us to fall into unhealthy patterns of behavior, self-denigrating thoughts, or dysfunctional relationships. We become defensive and unwilling to acknowledge responsibility for our own actions. We become arrogant and unable to admit our own weaknesses. We become impatient and reticent to recognize that everything really valuable in life unfolds slowly through processes that we may not be able to control. In these and thousands of other ways large and small, we fail to be the people that we most deeply are meant to be. In a word, we are in need of *teshuvah.*

To engage in *teshuvah,* psychologically speaking, is to come home to our truest selves. It is to cultivate profound self-awareness and do the inner work necessary to overcome all the fragmentation that prevents us from living fully. From this perspective, every transgression we commit is a symptom of some inner disarray, some part of ourselves that has not yet learned that our deepest satisfaction and happiness come only when we love ourselves fully and unequivocally, and then when we love others as we love ourselves. Using each moral failing as an opportunity to more fully explore our character defects, as genuine soul reckoning requires, involves committing ourselves to a lifelong process of struggling to know ourselves, even when that process leads us to painful realizations that we would prefer to brush aside.

Living in this way, of course, requires enormous courage. As Maslow put it:

> Self-knowledge seems to be the major path of self-improvement, though not the only one. Self-knowledge and self-improvement is very difficult for most people. It usually needs great courage and long struggle.[5]

Everyone who has struggled and stumbled along the path of *teshuvah* would recognize herself in that description.

Classical views of *teshuvah* confirm much of what humanistic psychologists have taught us about ourselves: that we are ultimately free and must be responsible for our own lives; that all of us have an innate drive toward self-realization and a desire to live fulfilling, meaningful lives; that doing so requires us to engage in ongoing self-scrutiny; and that our ultimate task in life is to become that self we truly are (in Rogers's words, below) or "holy, as God is holy" (in the words of Leviticus 19:2). Engaging in *teshuvah*, then, frees us to be ourselves, which is to be what God intended for us to be—people who live with integrity, responsibility, and wholeness. Rogers, perhaps unwittingly, describes the life of the penitent with uncanny accuracy when he writes:

> The individual moves toward *being*, knowingly and acceptingly, the process which he inwardly and actually *is*. He moves away from being what he is not, from being a facade. He is not trying to be more than he is, with the attendant feelings of insecurity or bombastic defensiveness. He is not trying to be less than he is, with the attendant feelings of guilt or self-depreciation. He is increasingly listening to the deepest recesses of his physiological and emotional being, and finds himself increasingly willing to be, with greater accuracy and depth, that self which he most truly is.... To be what he truly is, this is the path of life which he appears to value most highly, when he is free to move in any direction.[6]

25

The Dignity of Penitents

Just as a claim of fraud applies to buying and
   selling,
so a claim of fraud applies to spoken words.
One may not say, "How much is this object?"
if he does not want to buy it.
One may not say to a penitent, "Remember your
   former deeds."
Or to a convert, "Remember the deeds of your
   ancestors."

Mishnah, Baba Metzia **4:10**

Fraud comes in many forms. We typically think of fraud as a form of deceit for the purpose of stealing someone's property. Typically, a person makes representations or promises that are untrue and so induces another to pay for some good or service that he will never receive. The classic case might be the used car salesman who misrepresents the condition of the car so that the buyer will pay more than it is really worth. Bernard Madoff is the most infamous example of someone who told people he was investing money for them and sent them false monthly statements of their investment returns, when in fact he was using the money for his own benefit and not investing in anything at all. Fraud is a crime of stealing property, with the added element of deceit (as distinct from robbing someone by force or by stealth).

This mishnah's claim, then, is surprising. How could there be a case of purely verbal fraud? If someone doesn't actually take the other person's property, where's the fraud? And how are we to understand the juxtaposition of these three examples regarding the shopkeeper, the penitent, and the convert?

The concept that links these cases is what the mishnah calls "verbal oppression or coercion" (*ona'at d'varim*). The first case is most closely linked to commercial fraud and so is the easiest to grasp. If I pretend to be a potential buyer of something that I genuinely have no interest in purchasing, I deceive the seller. I mislead the shopkeeper by raising false expectations, only to deprive him of the sale he hoped to make. In this way, I steal his hope and replace it with disappointment. What I take from him is intangible rather than material, but it is real nonetheless, and the loss is every bit as real. Moreover, my motivation for deceiving the seller may be to gain information, say, about the going price of some product, so that I can then drive a better bargain with some other merchant. So I am stealing a piece of knowledge from this merchant to better my position. The Rabbis recognized that this form of deceit results in a loss no less than the monetary loss perpetrated by fraud. It is a forbidden form of verbal oppression.

But how is this principle relevant to the issue of reminding penitents or converts of their former lives? In both these cases, people have left their pasts behind and begun new lives. They have acquired a new sense of self and with it a renewed sense of hope for the future. This new status brings with it a sense of honor and dignity, as well as an expectation of being accepted by the community they have joined (or rejoined). In some significant way, both penitents and converts are new people with new identities.

Reminding such people of their pasts deprives them of this dignity and replaces it with denigration. It is degrading and disrespectful to remind penitents of their former misdeeds, because it steals from them what they have worked so hard to attain—a fresh start in life. This use of language is oppressive, for it forcibly wrests from people their pride and self-esteem.

The motivation behind doing this might be quite similar to that of the customer feigning a desire to buy. Degrading others, especially by calling attention to a part of their past of which they might be ashamed, is a way of building up our own egos. It gives us a comparative feeling of superiority to "put down" someone else. And so in a very real if intangible way, this behavior steals something—dignity, honor, esteem—from another so that we can appear to have more of it.

It is no wonder, then, that medieval writers frequently recommended that penitents change their name. In Maimonides' words, "As if to say, 'I am other than who I was. I am no longer the same person who did those deeds'" (*Mishneh Torah*, Laws of Repentance 2:4). Taking a new name is a tangible and powerful symbol of claiming a new identity. It literally gives penitents a new reputation and enables them to reclaim their dignity. For penitents are, in every important sense, genuinely new people. Penitents have so fully disavowed their pasts that in a very real way it ceases to exist. And with a different past, the penitent really does have a new sense of identity. To call penitents by their old names or, what amounts to the same thing, to dredge up the misdeeds of their former selves, is to deny everything that they have achieved. It is to mistake them for the wrong person.

26

Reconciliation and Divine Forgiveness

For transgressions committed between an individual and the Omnipresent, the Day of
Atonement atones.
For transgressions between one individual and
another,
the Day of Atonement atones only if the one will
regain the goodwill of his fellow.

Mishnah, Yoma 8:9

We know that the Day of Atonement is the holiest day of the Jewish calendar, the day on which the community as a whole stands before God and asks for atonement from all its transgressions. It is a day devoted to fasting and confessional prayers, recounting the ancient Temple rituals of atonement and rituals of self-denial. The Torah indicates that God has given Israel this day precisely to cleanse it from all its sins: "For on this day shall atonement be made for you, to cleanse you; from all your sins you shall be clean before the LORD" (Leviticus 16:30). Yet for all its austere power, the Day of Atonement has limited effect. The Rabbis subtly subvert the plain meaning of the biblical text—this day will cleanse you from only *some* of your sins, it seems.

Why these limits on the efficaciousness of Yom Kippur? Surely, given that sins against others are also sins against God, God should be able to forgive them directly. And given that the Day of Atonement is supposed to cleanse Israel completely, why

118

should this particular category of transgressions be set apart and forgiveness for them be made contingent upon the goodwill of the individual harmed?

There is a profound message here about the nature of our transgressions against others. Our sins against others may indeed offend God, but they remain first and foremost offenses against our fellow human beings. The harm we do to God, or to our relationship with God, is distinctly secondary. This stands in contrast to that view of sin according to which its main effect is alienation from God and the main remedy, therefore, is asking forgiveness from God. On that view, we can and must seek to repair our relationship with God first and then work to undo the harm we have done to our neighbors. Such is the assumption underlying the classic Christian sacrament of penance, according to which the priest, acting as an instrument of God's grace, can forgive sinners for transgressions (mortal sins) committed against others. Sinners need only be truly remorseful and openly confess their transgressions to the priest, who offers divine absolution.[7]

Judaism, by contrast, teaches that the person seeking absolution cannot bypass the neighbor and appeal directly to God. These offenses are irreducibly moral—they fall squarely in the category of our interrelationships with our neighbors—and even God cannot, or will not, interfere in the process of reconciling one person to another. God's forgiveness will be granted if and only if the offender has first sought out the person harmed and made appropriate amends, and then only after the offended party has forgiven the offender. This is the idea that must have been on the mind of the author of the Gospel of Matthew when he wrote:

> So if you are offering your gift at the altar, and there remember that your brother has something against you, leave your gift there before the altar and go; first be reconciled to your brother, and then come and offer your gift.
>
> **(Matthew 5:23–24)**

There can be no strictly religious solutions to moral failings. Neither the priest nor the altar nor the Day of Atonement has the power to cleanse us if we have not first repaired the breaches in our relationships with others.

This way of understanding transgression and atonement places extraordinary power in the hands of the offended party. She holds the key to the offender's atonement on both the human and the divine levels. For the offender is beholden to the very person she harmed and must win her forgiveness through genuine expressions of contrition and restitution. Moreover, even God waits for the offended person's signal that the time is right for absolution. Why should the person harmed wield such power over the offender? There is something quite counterintuitive about this. We might suppose that because the perpetrator singlehandedly created the harm, she should be able to undo it. The offender didn't need the acquiescence of the other to create the problem, so why is that person's active involvement necessary to resolve it?

Here we discover the paradox at the heart of immoral behavior where the power relationships are precisely the opposite of what they would seem to be. When we hurt others with words or deeds, we are exercising a kind of power over them. Sometimes this is quite blatant, as when one person threatens another with physical violence. More frequently we simply use words in ways that we know will strike an emotional blow, and in doing so, we exert a kind of power over those we are talking to. But the moral effect (as distinct from the physical or emotional effect) of these transgressions is to place the injured party in the position of greater power. For now that person is entitled to something that has been taken from him—his safety or his dignity, perhaps. To be a victim of injustice is to gain the upper hand in the moral interaction, for the victim is entitled to exact a kind of moral compensation for the wrongs done to him. The offended party, then, gains a claim against the offender in direct proportion to the severity of the physical or psychological offense against him.

The resulting paradox is twofold: whatever power offenders wield on one level they lose on another, and the only way for them to achieve atonement for the offense is to win over the very people they harmed. There is but one road back to a state of moral equilibrium, to wholeness and a "clean record," and that road is controlled by the people who have been hurt. Because they are the ones who have been deprived of what was rightfully theirs, they are the ones who must acquiesce to any process of reconciliation. This sort of moral transaction was played out most dramatically in the Truth and Reconciliation Commission hearings in South Africa. There the perpetrators of violence under the apartheid regime were asked to publically confess their crimes, and the victims retained the power to forgive them and, in effect, reinstate them as members of society in good standing. But the same moral logic applies whether the offenses are monstrous or trivial. The key to undoing the harm done does not lie with the offender but with those who have been hurt. Even God cannot circumvent the moral calculus that governs our interactions with others, for doing so would deprive victims of their moral claim and deny offenders the opportunity for moral growth that comes only when they must face those they have hurt and humbly ask for their forgiveness.

27

Teshuvah of Love versus *Teshuvah* of Fear

Resh Lakish said, "Great is penitence, because it reduces one's deliberate sins to mere errors." But did not Resh Lakish say at another time, "Great is penitence, because it transforms one's deliberate sins into merits"? There is no difficulty here: the latter statement refers to penitence out of love, the former to penitence out of fear.

Babylonian Talmud, *Yoma* **86b**

Here is one of several instances in which the Sages of the Talmud distinguish penitence out of love and penitence out of fear. But what is really the difference between these, and why would these two kinds of penitence have such different effects?

The Rabbis' meaning here is somewhat elusive. Much depends on the unanswered question: fear (or love) of what? As we consider a few of the possibilities, we come to realize that the Rabbis' simple distinction is not so simple after all.

Most obviously, some people are motivated to repent for fear of being caught and punished for their transgression. Feelings of remorse and expressions of apology come more naturally when we are faced with the imminent prospect of having to pay the price for our misdeeds. Some of this may be self-serving and even disingenuous. Not many people are moved by expressions of remorse from someone whose criminal behavior continued over a period of decades. But sometimes this sort of remorse represents a genuine change of heart—the fear of punishment jolts a person, breaks through her self-deception, and causes her to take stock of her life in a new way.

But there is a different sort of fear that may motivate the penitent. A person will sometimes look at the choices he has made and the ways in which his behavior has undermined relationships, led to guilt and even self-loathing, and experiences of profound fear about the life he is leading. This sort of fear arises occasionally among hardened criminals and addicts who "hit bottom" and discover that they have so degraded themselves that they are literally afraid of how entrapped they have become in patterns of transgression. It is as though, after years of befriending sin, they suddenly discover a fear of sin that forces them to turn themselves around and head in a new direction.

But penitents can also be motivated by love—the love of God, or of righteousness, or of fellow human beings. Many of us know people like this. They seem to be generous and hospitable, compassionate and forgiving, by nature. It is as if they are drawn by a kind of magnetic force toward doing what is right. They are drawn toward positive behaviors just as consistently as others seem to be drawn to negative ones. This is not to suggest that such pious individuals never struggle to overcome the influence of their "evil inclination," only that they have cultivated a deep desire to orient their lives toward what is good. Such people are perpetually engaged in doing *teshuvah*, not because they have so much to repent for, but paradoxically because they are so focused on the love of God and neighbor that even their smallest shortcomings demand their attention.

It seems, then, that the fundamental distinction invoked by the Rabbis is between a repulsion by what we have done (or become) versus an attraction to the best of what we might be. This is consistent, of course, with their view that people live suspended between their evil inclination and their good inclination, always inclining toward one end of the moral spectrum or the other. It is not surprising, then, that they imagine two types of *teshuvah*, the one motivated by fear when the evil inclination has run rampant, the other motivated by love when the good inclination has taken root.

From the Rabbis' perspective, there is no bad reason for doing *teshuvah*. Whatever our motivation, when we set out to turn our lives again toward God and God's commandments, we are engaged in holy work. Perhaps this is why they insist that the gates of repentance are always open (Lamentations Rabbah 3:43). Repentance is always available—for those who are righteous and for those who are wicked, for those motivated by fear no less than for those motivated by love.

But it does not follow that all forms of repentance are created equal, as it were. For those of us motivated by fear, remorse is the driving force. We see what we have done or gaze into the abyss that we are falling into, and we feel genuine regret for the mistakes we have made. For those of us motivated by love, on the other hand, serving God ever more fully is the driving force. We realize that each error presents us with an opportunity to grow morally and so redeem a part of ourselves that until now has sometimes led us astray.

So it is that repentance of fear and repentance of love have different consequences. The former, in Resh Lakish's view, turns intentional sins into unintentional ones. For once we truly regret our transgressions, the deliberate, willful quality of them can be set aside. We are left with a simple mistake, a lapse of judgment, something we now wish we had never done, and so our current intention to do good in effect replaces our former intention to do wrong. Repentance of love, however, has more far-reaching effects. By turning each transgression we commit into a new opportunity to serve God more fully, we raise those transgressions, in effect, into merits.

Both types of repentance are transformative of the individual penitent. Both result in moral renewal and involve a turning from one course of action to another. But the repentance of fear, motivated as it is by the circumstances in which we find ourselves, can alter only the circumstances surrounding the transgression; what was deliberate now becomes unintentional. Only the repentance of love, motivated by the desire to grow ever closer to God, has the power to transform our transgressions into merits, for the sin itself has now become the impetus to cleave to truth and righteousness.

28

Returning to the Source

The primary role of penitence, which at once
sheds light on the darkened zone, is for the person to return to himself, to the root of his soul.
Then he will at once return to God, to the Soul of
all souls.... It is only through the great truth of
returning to oneself that the person and the
people, the world and all the worlds, the whole
of existence, will return to their Creator, to be
illumined by the light of life.

Rabbi Abraham Isaac Kook[8]

Insofar as *teshuvah* means "to return," most often we think of
this as returning to the straight path, the way of righteousness,
after straying. But there is a deeper sense of return that Rabbi
Kook, the first chief rabbi of Israel, captures in the above quotation. In a profound sense, *teshuvah* entails a return to our truest
selves and also to God, to the godliness within us. What does this
mean, and which dimensions of *teshuvah* does it reveal besides the
psychological and moral aspects that we have already explored?

We can begin by turning to a traditional prayer recited by
Jews every day at the very beginning of the morning service:

My God, the soul which You have placed within me is pure.
You have created it, You have formed it, You have breathed it
into me.

The nature of the soul is a very complex religious question, one that
we cannot explore here in detail. But whatever else we believe the

125

soul to be, it represents the element of the Divine within us. And because the word for "soul" in Hebrew is *neshamah*, which is closely connected with breath, we might reasonably infer that the soul is that life force in us that makes us living, breathing, animate beings. Indeed, the prayer cited on the previous page goes on to thank God for restoring our soul to us each morning, on the assumption that sleep is akin to death and so awakening is a reenlivening of our lifeless bodies.

In this sense, we all sometimes lose a connection to our souls, not only when we sleep (and typically lose awareness of our breathing), but also when we ignore the divine source of our lives. Often we sleepwalk through life, doing our daily tasks and managing quite nicely, but quite unaware of the divine energy animating our lives. We are asleep in just the way that American author and poet Henry David Thoreau complained about when he explained what motivated him to go live in the woods: "To be awake is to be alive. I have never yet met a man who was quite awake. How could I have looked him in the face?"[9] To be fully awake and alive is to be in touch with the Source of our lives, the miracle that we are alive at all, and the force that sustains us moment by moment.

The Rabbis understood this idea of being alive to our souls in a moral, as well as a metaphysical, sense. They wrote, "The righteous in death are called 'alive,' while the wicked, even while alive, are called 'dead'" (Babylonian Talmud, *Berakhot* 18a). One way of understanding this is that the lives of the righteous continue to enhance the lives of others long after they have died, while the wicked rob others of their lives even while they are still alive. In another sense, though, the point might be about the ways in which we are (or aren't) in touch with our own souls.

When we live righteously, we are deeply connected to God, grateful for the gift of our lives, and aware that we are accountable to God for what we make of our lives. For the Rabbis, who believed in an afterlife, this connection to God continued after death; indeed, the primary reward for living righteously in this world, in their view, is that we continue to live in God's presence in the next world. Sinners, on the other hand, live disconnected from their own divine nature and from a sense of accountability to God. In that sense, they live "dead," soulless lives, oblivious to the moral purpose with which God has invested our lives.

Doing *teshuvah*, then, is about reclaiming our connection to that divine source of our lives. We have experienced the sense of alienation from our deepest selves that leaves us feeling empty, morally deficient, and spiritually deadened. When we reassert that there is divine purpose to our lives, we awaken to a new sense of being alive and to the awareness of how each day can be an opportunity to live more soulfully, and more morally.

The purity of our souls is there, waiting to be rediscovered. The transgressions we have committed may burden us, but they do not have the power to transform the essence of who we are. As Rabbi Soloveitchik wrote:

> It is a cornerstone for Judaism, emphasized especially in Hassidism and in the Kabbalah, that however great a man's transgressions may be, they fail to penetrate to the innermost core of his soul. Always, and under all circumstances, there remains something pure, precious, and sacred in man's soul.[10]

Engaging in *teshuvah* brings us home to our truest selves and, so too, to the Divine within us. To return to our Creator in this way is, in Kook's poetic formulation, "to be illumined by the light of life."

Part V

Experiencing *Teshuvah*

29

A Theological Virtue

The disposition of the heart is part of virtue.

Phillipa Foot[1]

At least since the time of Aristotle, Western ethicists have attempted to identify and explain the particular character traits that define a virtuous life. The classical virtues were prudence (sometimes understood as wisdom), temperance, fortitude, and justice. These traits were understood to be innate, in the sense that the capacity to cultivate them is intrinsic to human life, and universal, in that all people in all times and places will find that these traits lead to human happiness and social harmony. These four virtues were supplemented by three more religious virtues: faith, hope, and love (or charity), which were understood to be specific gifts of God, based on Paul's writings in 1 Corinthians 13:13. Both the "cardinal" and the "theological" virtues were commonly understood to entail a kind of discernment, an ability to determine the ends that we ought to pursue and the means by which we achieve them. Learning to live a virtuous life was taken to be a lifelong endeavor demanding sustained effort; no one becomes virtuous by accident or haphazardly.

The capacity to repent might also be regarded as a sort of virtue. The capacity to do *teshuvah* may be regarded as innate, and yet it requires considerable effort and often years of practice to cultivate it. Like the classical virtues, doing *teshuvah* is very much about discerning the proper goals of human life and the way to progress toward them. And like a virtue-oriented ethic, which defines the good in terms of character development,

131

teshuvah is primarily about the continual re-creation of ourselves through the cultivation of certain moral capacities, or virtues. I believe that, in fact, *teshuvah* encompasses several specific virtues and that these, taken together, are necessary for successful repentance.

But, like the so-called "Christian" virtues of faith, hope, and love, repentance is also very much about cultivating a relationship with God. We engage in *teshuvah* when we become aware that we have strayed from that relationship and need to return. The capacity to "turn" is often experienced as a kind of Divine Presence in our lives in its own right, and certainly the result of doing *teshuvah* is that we strengthen our connection to the Divine, however we may experience it.

Understood in this way, *teshuvah* encompasses both moral and theological virtue. Like the classical virtues of prudence and fortitude, it shapes our behavior toward others; like the theological virtues of faith and hope, it directs our spiritual lives toward what is ultimate, beyond the human realm. Indeed, the special significance of *teshuvah* in Jewish moral life lies precisely in the way it links these two dimensions of our experience. *Teshuvah* reminds us that moral development and renewal occur in the context of renewing our relationship with God. Moral "turning" and spiritual "turning" are part of an integrated whole, so that the best (perhaps the only) way to overcome our moral failings is to reawaken to certain spiritual realities.

So it should come as no surprise that the need for repentance, and the call to engage in this moral/spiritual work, is embedded in the structure of Jewish liturgy. Daily the words of Jewish prayer remind us that we have sinned, that we are in need of moral rehabilitation and divine forgiveness, and that we seek God's help in doing this difficult work of purifying our hearts:

> Bring us back to Your Torah, our Father, and draw us near to Your service, and return us to You in perfect repentance. Blessed are You, Lord, who desires repentance.

> Forgive us, Father, for we have sinned, pardon us for we have transgressed, for You forgive and pardon. Blessed are You, Lord, gracious and abundantly forgiving.

Because if, as the Greek philosophers taught, virtue is about directing our will toward the right ends, predisposing our hearts to love, prudence, justice, and all the rest, then Judaism would add that we must "direct our hearts toward God" (Babylonian Talmud, *Berakhot* 17a). Virtue, the cultivation of human moral excellence, cannot be divorced from piety, the cultivation of intimacy with the Divine. Doing *teshuvah*, then, requires that we break down the distinction between moral and theological virtues and so enables us to live simultaneously in a way that is both good and godly.

30

Devotion to Truthfulness

As individuals, we can come before the Holy Seat
of the All-knowing and the All-judging, bringing
with us only the simple, naked truth.
Rabbi Joseph B. Soloveitchik[2]

Telling the simple, naked truth is often anything but simple. All of us stretch the truth from time to time, or simply fail to disclose the full truth about something, and most of us are prone to at least occasional bald-faced lies. We can safely ignore "white lies," falsehoods we tell to protect the feelings of others, which are sometimes essential to maintaining graceful social relations. The real problem concerns those departures from the truth that are deliberate attempts to prevent others from knowing what we've done or who we are. Deception of one sort or another has been a part of human experience since the beginning of recorded time. It is also the first roadblock on the path to real soul reckoning and *teshuvah*.

Why do we lie, and how could we begin to overcome our tendency to do so? When we look closely at those times when we say something false, I think we discover that the motivation is generally to cover over some real or perceived failing. We have missed a deadline for a work assignment and don't want to face the consequences from our boss, so we say we were never informed about the date or that we were misinformed. We forgot to do something we had promised for our partner, and rather than deal with the angry or disappointed response, we make excuses by inventing some distraction or conflict, so that our failure is somehow not fully our responsibility. Or in the midst of a dispute with a friend, we tell a story that reflects only part of the truth, conveniently ignoring the details that would cast our behavior in a negative light.

In myriad ways, we are prone to making ourselves look better, sometimes even just marginally better, than we really are. We do this, I think, because we feel we will lose some of our power in relation to others if they know "the simple, naked truth." Sometimes this is as simple as a loss of their approval. Sometimes it may have more tangible consequences, such as loss of money, a relationship, or a job. But, whatever the circumstances, lying is meant to hide the truth from others in order to protect us—our prestige, our lovableness, our resources—and so retain some measure of personal power that we might otherwise lose.

Seen in this light, we can appreciate why lying comes so easily, and why it is so seductive. Lying is attractive because, in many instances, it works—that is, as long as we are not discovered. If we can hide our blemishes from the sight of others, it is as though they really don't exist. By lying, we can control the perceptions others have of us, and so make reality different, at least in the eyes of those we lie to, at least as long as they don't uncover our deception. And this is why we sometimes find it virtually irresistible to compound our lying. For if someone is on to us, we may feel the only practical course of action is to invent a second lie to cover up the first. After all, the whole point of lying is to cover up the truth, and the original fabrication will fail to achieve its goal if it is not reinforced. And, having already started down the path of dishonesty, the first deceptive step only makes the second or third step that much easier to take.

This entire complex of feelings, goals, and strategies must be dismantled in order to begin to cultivate devotion to truthfulness. But how can we uproot a tendency so deeply rooted in human nature? The answer, I think, lies in a spiritual reorientation of our lives. In a word, we need to think less of our relationship to others and pay closer attention to our relationship to God.

In the final analysis, our desire to lie is directly tied to our desire to control the way others see us, and this desire, in turn, stems from an effort to protect whatever advantage we gain from appearing to be better than we really are. It follows that the only way to break this cycle of deception is to detach ourselves from this goal. We can begin by asking ourselves to imagine a situation in which we would be inclined to lie—perhaps a time when we have actually done so—and then consider the possibility of telling the truth instead. What do we stand to lose? How difficult is it to imagine accepting that loss as the real-life consequence of our misdeeds, whatever they were? Once we begin to consider that we could live with those consequences, that they will not kill us, then we have taken the first step toward loosening our attachment to controlling the way others perceive us.

But breaking a tendency to lie and developing a devotion to truthfulness are two different things. To do the latter, we will need to replace a concern for others' perceptions with a concern for how God perceives us. Elsewhere I have noted that *teshuvah* can be understood at least partly as a process of coming to see ourselves as God sees us. But the point is also that we need to *care* about how God sees us more than about how friends, co-workers, and even family members see us. If we live a God-centered life—and surely repenting is about putting the Divine, however we conceive it, at the center of our lives—then we can set aside our habitual concerns to please others. For when we cultivate a devotion to God alone, we are concerned above all to make our peace with the simple, naked truth of our lives.

All this requires a kind of trust that even if we lose the approval of others, we will be fundamentally right in the only way that counts. Nurturing that sort of trust is one of the virtues essential to doing *teshuvah*, which, as we know, is a spiritual path as much as a moral one. Truthfulness must become for us not just an option, but a habit, and then an essential component of our lives. The Rabbis said simply, "The seal of God is truth" (Song of Songs Rabbah 1:9). When devotion to truthfulness is our highest priority, it becomes our seal, as well.

31

Cultivating Humility

Humility is the root and beginning of repentance.

Bachya ibn Pakuda[3]

There are those among us who can never admit they have done wrong. They adamantly resist the suggestion that they are to blame. When confronted with the evidence of their errors, they resort to defensiveness and even counterattack. They seem to live surrounded by a kind of psychic armor that prevents criticism—in extreme cases, even mild criticism—from penetrating. They might admit in theory that, of course, they are not perfect. But, in practice, they cannot own up to any mistakes. Their problem is an excess of pride.

Pride stands in the way of honest self-examination and self-disclosure. Indeed, it impedes the process of *teshuvah* as it has been described here at every stage. It prevents us from taking responsibility for what we have done, which is the very first step on the path of *teshuvah*. But then it also closes the door to feelings of remorse. It won't tolerate public confession or apology. It is ultimately opposed to soul reckoning, to say nothing of inner transformation. Pride may not be the root of all evil, but it may well be the one vice that more than any other precludes us from doing the work of *teshuvah*.

Most distressingly, when we are really honest with ourselves, we recognize that we are all guilty of pridefulness, at least in some measure, at least occasionally. How, then, are we to combat pride? Or, perhaps more helpfully, how do we cultivate its opposite, humility?

Medieval Rabbis offered much advice about how to reorient ourselves to instill in us feelings of modesty. Often this involves contemplating our true place in the order of nature. Bachya ibn Pakuda, a rabbi from eleventh-century Spain, puts it starkly:

> When one thinks of the transient character of his existence, how swiftly death comes, at which time his desires and hopes are cut off and he must leave all his possessions and relinquish the idea that he can take any of them as provision for the hereafter, or that any of these will be of use to him when he is in the grave—the light of his countenance gone, its brightness dimmed, his body breeding worms, turning into corruption and deliquescence, the marks of his physical beauty vanished, the corpse emitting an increasingly foul odour, as if it had never been washed or cleansed or emitted a pleasant odour—when these and similar considerations enter his mind, he will become humble and lowly. He will not be proud. His heart will not uplift itself arrogantly.[4]

Such advice will strike most of us as extreme, perhaps even ridiculous. But if we think about it for just a moment, we will realize just how much wisdom Bachya offers us here. In our pride, we cling to an image of ourselves as invincible, unblemished, and superior to others. But the reality of our lives, and especially of our inevitable deaths, conveys another message, if only we will listen to it. Attending to that message thoroughly undermines our self-importance and self-righteousness at the most fundamental level. And it is from that place that we are ready to engage in *teshuvah*.

The effect of cultivating humility is that it brings us back into a dynamic relationship with ourselves and those around us. Where we had previously been cut off from others by the armor of self-aggrandizement and even self-delusion, humility puts our lives back into proper perspective. Where pride precluded us from feeling remorse and so from taking steps to improve ourselves, humility opens us to the possibility of our own growth, for it allows us to see our shortcomings and resolve to overcome them. Pride leads to an ossified, static life; humility opens our hearts and enables us to embrace change, and changing is the essence of *teshuvah*.

We can foster humility in ourselves in less jarring ways than those suggested by Bachya. We can read literature that stimulates us to self-reflection. We can develop a practice of sitting quietly and journaling about the events of our lives, our regrets, and our goals. We can search out people who seem to us to exemplify the quality of humility and pay close attention to how they carry themselves in the world. But, however we choose to cultivate it, humility is the first essential virtue of the penitent.

32

God's Role in *Teshuvah*

God said to them, "It depends upon you, as it is
said,
'Return unto Me, and I will return unto you'
(Malachi 3:7)."
The community spoke before God, "LORD of the
universe,
it depends upon You, as it is said,
'Restore us, O God of our salvation' (Psalm 85:5)."
Therefore it is said, "Turn us unto Thee, O LORD,
and we shall be turned" (Lamentations 5:21).
Lamentations Rabbah 5:21

The work of repentance is not a solitary undertaking. This passage from Lamentations Rabbah and many others like it point
toward a partnership between the penitent and God, who supports this transformational process. But why should this be so?
Surely the transgressor didn't need any divine help to commit
these hurtful actions. Why are we capable of "screwing up" on
our own but seem to need God's help to put ourselves right again?

Of course, almost all accounts of repentance assume that
most of the work of moral transformation falls to the penitent.
Certainly the dimension of repentance that involves absolution
from God must be initiated by the transgressor, whether in the
form of sacrifices, prayers, or other efforts to win divine forgiveness. And the work of reconciliation with those we've harmed is
only meaningful and can only succeed in repairing these relationships when we ourselves offer apologies and restitution. But these

efforts—and perhaps especially the aspect of this work that takes place in the recesses of our souls and in the privacy of our own thoughts—need divine assistance to be truly effective.

The reasons for this may lie in the nature of sin and in the arduous process of moral rehabilitation itself. With each transgression that we commit, we find ourselves more deeply entrenched in our moral failings. In the words of Ben Azzai, one of the Sages of the Mishnah, "One transgression leads to another" (*Pirkei Avot* 4:2). The negative things we do have a certain momentum of their own (as do the positive things we do, which the Rabbis likewise realized). The first time someone cheats a client, there is almost certainly some hesitation and subsequent guilt. But with each successive offense, the inner resistance to cheating weakens until finally it becomes routine.

This isn't just a matter of habit, like getting stuck in a pattern of self-destructive behavior, such as smoking or drug use. There is a psychological process whereby we are prone to justifying the transgressions we commit. The more routine they become, the more likely we are to justify our conduct. It is as though we defend ourselves from what would otherwise be a mounting sense of guilt and shame by convincing ourselves that our transgressions are not really transgressions at all, or at least they are not as serious as we once (rightly) assumed. This is the deep psychological reality that the Rabbis captured when they said, "When a man has committed a transgression and repeated it, it has become permissible to him" (Babylonian Talmud, *Kiddushin* 40b). In our minds, we turn the prohibited into the permissible, which in turn makes it easier to do what is prohibited yet again.

But there is another sense in which we are mired in sinfulness, a sense that we often overlook when we focus exclusively on individual transgressions. Sinfulness is a condition that affects our will and that is embedded in our nature. It is about how we are oriented, as well as what we do. The desire to seek my own good, even when I know that doing so involves trampling on the legitimate needs and rights of others; the predisposition to exaggerate my own merits while downplaying those of others; the tendency to place something material or transitory—wealth, success, prestige, or power—at the center of my concern; the penchant to underestimate the very seriousness of these forces working within me and so give them even freer rein—all these are aspects of sinfulness at work within us. For in truth we are morally flawed creatures. This is the reality that Christians have long recognized when they insist that sin is an existential reality, something that perverts our will, leading us both to seek what we should rather avoid and to obscure the very goods that we should pursue.[5]

In this view, of course, it makes perfect sense to assume that we are incapable of extricating ourselves from sin. Given that we are prone to misidentifying sinful choices as acceptable, and also to succumbing to temptation even when we recognize the immoral course of action for what it is, how can we depend on ourselves to do the work of freeing ourselves from the grips of our own moral incapacities? Sin exerts something akin to the gravitational pull of the earth, only in the moral rather than the physical sphere. It is acting upon us, holding us down, even when we are not conscious of it. It constrains our movement, making it difficult (albeit not impossible) to free ourselves from its powerful pull. To the extent that the forces of good within us are counterbalanced by forces of evil, we do well not to rely entirely on our own goodwill to motivate us to repent. For, if we are honest with ourselves, we know that there are equally powerful forces at work within us that will avoid, subvert, or negate the work of repentance.

So it is that we reach out to a higher source of goodness and blessing—which need not be understood in traditionally theistic terms—to assist us. We need help to purify our intentions, recognize when we are in the grips of self-deception, and give us the perseverance to continue on the path of repentance. We need help sometimes even to recognize that we need help, that we cannot do this alone. All of this accounts for the many prayers in which we beseech God to support us in our work of repentance.

God's intervention in the process of repentance may be needed in yet another way, to bolster our sense of self-worth in the face of our transgressions and believe that repentance is even a possibility. For some, transgression brings in its wake a profound sense of shame and self-deprecation. The pridefulness and self-aggrandizement that were exhibited in flagrant transgressions are now reversed, and the wrongdoer now finds that it is impossible to believe in a new beginning at all. The mistakes of the past preclude any possibility of redemption. And if there is no way forward, no chance to begin anew, then the way to repentance is blocked before it even begins. To be infected with such a sense of moral worthlessness is to be in a place entirely unreachable by the hopeful message that repentance is available.

For we know that doing the work of repentance depends on the prior belief in the possibility of repentance. And this, in turn, is a matter of hope and faith that we are not enslaved to the past. In this sense, our transgressions can themselves be the greatest impediment to our repenting for them, because they can deprive us of the very hope we need to disavow the past and "turn" in a different direction. They immobilize us, making us feel that we have nowhere to turn, that any effort we might make is ultimately futile. That feeling of desperation and helplessness may be countered only with a ray of hope that finds its way into our lives from some source outside us.

And so we find many prayers asking that we be freed from shame, which is the feeling that we are unworthy of redemption. We need some divine assurance that there is, indeed, a way forward, for we ourselves have lost touch with that reality. If we can come to believe that forgiveness is a possibility, that God will take us back despite our moral failings, then all is not lost after all. Therefore, we pray to have our hearts opened to that message of hope that can come to us only from somewhere beyond our own experience. The psalmist cries out, "I said, 'LORD be gracious to me, heal me, for I have sinned against You'" (Psalm 41:5).

Repentance, then, depends in some measure on God's work in our lives, helping us seek out and pursue the good and affirming the possibility that the path to repentance is available to us. The individual journey of repentance recapitulates the national experience of liberation from slavery, for in fact it is a version of the same struggle. Like the Israelites in Egypt, we need to be able to break free from complacency and awaken to the fact that we are in need of liberation. First, we have to believe that such liberation is more than an idealized goal; it is a genuine possibility. Then we need the courage to pursue that goal even when we revert to our former slave mentality. And finally, we need the imagination to create a new life in which we carry with us the remembrance that "we were slaves to Pharaoh in Egypt" (Deuteronomy 6:21), even as we create a new life as free people obligated to serve God. The Israelites did not persevere in this long, arduous process through their own efforts alone, though the Rabbis were clear that they needed to take the first, decisive steps in their long march to freedom. Rather, as the biblical text repeatedly emphasizes, it was "with a strong hand and an outstretched arm" (Deuteronomy 26:8) that God liberated them. So, too, we hope that each time we turn again toward a life of righteousness, we can rely on God's assistance in tandem with our own efforts to bring about healing and transformation.

33

One Day Ahead

Rabbi Eliezer said, "Repent one day before your death." His disciples asked him, "Does then one know on what day he will die?" "All the more reason he should repent today, lest he die tomorrow."

Babylonian Talmud, *Shabbat* **53a**

When is the right time to repent? The assumption behind Eliezer's view would seem to be that the optimal time is as close to the time of our death as possible. If the idea is that repentance negates our transgressions, then repenting at the last possible moment will ensure that we die with a clean slate, so to speak, with no outstanding sins on our record. From this perspective, the rabbi's advice would seem to be simple common sense. Because we can't be certain of when we will die—and this must have been even truer in a time when the state of medical care was more primitive than it is today—we'd better repent every single day. But there is more here than just pragmatic advice.

Repenting, as we have seen, entails a whole series of steps and requires deep soul reckoning. It would seem, then, that we can repent only when we are truly ready, when external circumstances have forced us to confront the severity of our transgressions, or when we have reached a level of self-awareness that enables us to probe our shortcomings honestly and fully. If repentance is to be more than pro forma, a matter of going through the motions, then we need to wait until the time is right. Repentance, it would seem, is not the sort of thing that we can do on a predetermined schedule.

Thinking of repentance in this way is very much in line with the spirit of our times. Our culture tends to value subjective experience over conformity to externally imposed standards. We want our religious lives especially to be meaningful, an expression of our deepest desires and feelings, not a matter of fulfilling an obligation. We should pray when we feel moved to pray, apologize when we feel truly sorry, give charity when we are genuinely moved by the plight of the poor. Doing the "right" thing, but without the proper intent, strikes most of us as empty at best and perhaps even hypocritical.

Judaism, however, has always placed an emphasis on proper action first, with the understanding that human emotion is fickle and unreliable. The poor need to be fed whether we are feeling particularly generous or stingy on any given day. As Abraham Joshua Heschel, philosopher and theologian, taught with respect to prayer, *kavanah* (proper intention) may follow from *keva* (proper ritual behavior).[6] We need the routine of set times for prayer in order to cultivate the spiritual sensibilities that make prayer meaningful. If we simply wait for the need to arise in us spontaneously, it may never happen.

The same is true for *teshuvah*. Precisely because repenting is such hard work, we will naturally avoid it if we don't practice it regularly. Like every endeavor in which we strive for excellence— think of professional athletes or musicians—we become more proficient when we adopt a rigorous training regimen. Our spiritual lives are no different. It's not just that "practice makes perfect." It's that without regular practice, the motivation to strive for improvement wanes. We get lazy. We procrastinate. We make excuses that we can have a meaningful spiritual life without working at it. But if we take a moment to reflect honestly, we know that we are fooling ourselves.

Hence the importance of repenting every day. We become more proficient and more motivated when we are habituated to the practice of doing *teshuvah*. But if this were Eliezer's only point, then why not just say, "Repent every day"? Why does he say instead, "Repent one day before your death"?

The awareness of our mortality is the ground of our spirituality. When we focus even for a moment on the inevitability of our death, on the fact that one day we will leave this world and "return to dust," we are reminded of our fragility and our vulnerability. And this is precisely the mindset in which we can approach those we have hurt in a spirit of humility and make amends to them. When we keep awareness of death at bay and live our lives as though they will continue indefinitely, then we lose touch with the truth of our existence, and therefore the truth of our moral lives, the reality of our failings, and our dependence on the goodwill of others. Death awareness leads to moral and spiritual self-awareness, which are the preconditions of doing *teshuvah*.

If we consider deeply that this day might be our very last, then we will feel not only the urgency to repent in order to make sure we die with a clean record. We will also be cultivating each and every day an awareness of our weakness and moral frailty that makes repentance feel as natural and as necessary to our spiritual health as eating and breathing are to our physical health. Our mortality reminds us of the need to repent and of the ways in which repentance can make this time-bound life meaningful. "Repent one day before your death"—cultivate every day the awareness that death may be imminent, and certainly inevitable, and you will be drawn to the daily practice of *teshuvah*.

34

Seeing the Goodness

Know that you must judge everyone with an eye
to their merits. Even regarding those who are
completely wicked, one must search and find
some small way in which they are not wicked and
with respect to this bit of goodness, judge them
with an eye to their merits. In this way, one truly
elevates their merit and thereby encourages them
to do *teshuvah*.

Rabbi Nachman of Breslov, *Likutei Moharan* **282**

Finding the goodness in one another is harder than it sounds. For many of us, the tendency is rather to turn a critical eye to others and accentuate their shortcomings. This may be especially true for those of us who have highly developed analytical skills, for we have been educated to think critically about ideas and projects of all sorts. Our professional success may depend on our exercising these faculties regularly. It is entirely natural, then, when we apply these same judgmental attitudes to others. Moving ourselves and others along the path of repentance, however, may require exactly the opposite.

When we respond critically to others, especially if our criticism is accompanied by a harsh or an unforgiving tone, we tend to diminish their standing in our eyes, and even in their own. They are "less" than we assumed or expected—less competent, less honest, less reliable. Their faults are exposed, and they are found to be wanting. Our criticism of others frequently causes them to think less of themselves, particularly if we hold some power over them. In some circumstances our critique may even be devastating for their self-esteem and sense of well-being.

Of course, criticism of all sorts is essential to many relationships. Medical interns cannot be trained if the doctors overseeing them do not offer criticism; children cannot learn right from wrong unless their parents criticize their behavior, especially when they are very young; athletes cannot improve if their coaches do not critique their performance. But, as everyone who has conducted evaluations knows, criticism is most effective if we begin with words of praise. This is not only a matter of effective strategy, in that our critical words will hurt less if we affirm the recipient first. Rather, the point is that when we express our appreciation along with our criticism, we let others know that we see them as whole people, that we understand that they are more than their shortcomings. Then the criticism can be heard in the context of being "judged with an eye to their merits" and can be taken in without evoking feelings of shame.

Nachman's insight draws upon this experience of offering and receiving criticism. We are often motivated to do *teshuvah* after someone has made us aware of our mistakes. But at the same time, we need to believe in our ability to change, and this is possible only when we are in touch with our own goodness as well as our failings. When we recognize the goodness in others and judge them favorably (even when their transgressions are obvious), we invite them to see themselves in a more positive light and believe in the possibility of their own improvement.

Within my recovery circle, I have often listened as men shared their experiences of addiction. These are often painful, even wrenching, stories of abuse, self-destructive behaviors, deception, despair, and profound shame. After a speaker has shared his story, there is an opportunity for others in the group to respond. One member, Paul, always offers the same feedback. He says:

> I listened carefully to your story and I want you to know that nothing in what you shared makes me want to turn away from you. On the contrary, it makes me want to get to know you

better. You are a really good person, and your goodness really
shone through in the story you told about your experience.

The first few times I heard Paul respond in this way, I thought
either that he was naive or perhaps that he had been listening to
someone else. Goodness? All I heard was a series of broken promises, poor choices, and abusive behaviors. But in time I came to
realize that Paul was listening to something between the lines of the
story, something deeper than the words. He was listening for the
words of remorse and the voice of the speaker's conscience that were
a window into his soul. And there he could see clearly the essential goodness of a man whose life has been in shambles, and yet
who is yearning to find a healthier, sounder way of life. Paul's
feedback is often met with tears of relief and joy, as years of
shame begin to dissolve and the speaker begins to get in touch
again with his own inner goodness.

There is goodness in all of us, even, as Nachman says, those
we think of (or who think of themselves) as "completely wicked."
When that goodness is seen and affirmed by others, it enables us
to rediscover the goodness within ourselves, sometimes for the
first time in years. And as we focus on our capacity for goodness,
we begin to redefine who we are and recover our potential to live
lives of integrity. This is perhaps the most powerful step we can
take in the process of "turning."

We may be accustomed to viewing others critically, but it is
when we view them with an eye to their merits that we help
them claim their own potential for improvement. Seeing the
goodness in others, perhaps especially in those who cannot see it
themselves, is an extraordinary gift. It is often precisely the gift
they need to begin the process of *teshuvah*.

35

Faith in the Certainty
of Renewal

Let not man say, "I have sinned and there is no
hope for me," but let him put his confidence in the
Holy One, who is blessed, and he will be received.

Midrash, Psalms 40:3

Sometimes when we are deeply aware of our failings, we fall
into a state of despair. We have made a mess of our lives—
through irresponsible behavior toward our neighbors, deceit in
our professional lives, or dishonesty in our relationships with
loved ones. We live with a sense of shame, and nothing feels so
certain to us as the fact that we are beyond redemption.

Traditional Jewish Sages caution against such despair, for
they recognized that it is a major impediment to doing *teshuvah*.
For if our situation is genuinely hopeless, then there is certainly
no point in engaging in the difficult work of repentance. No
doubt, sometimes this sense of despair becomes a rationalization
for continuing along the path of transgression. In that way, the
belief in our hopelessness becomes a self-fulfilling prophecy.

We have to believe in the possibility of renewal before we
can take the steps necessary to bring it about. In this sense, faith
is at the very heart of repentance—faith in the possibility of a new
life, free of shame and guilt, without the burdens imposed by our
past mistakes. Rabbi Kook puts it best, "This is the entire basis of
penitence: the elevation of the will, and changing it to good, to go
out of darkness to light, from the valley of despair to the door of

hope."[7] But this is so much easier said than done. How can we find that sort of faith where it doesn't exist?

There are surely no easy formulas for creating hope. But some words of wisdom have come down to us from earlier generations of rabbis. Nachman of Breslov, the Hasidic master, was quoted as saying, "If you believe you have the power to ruin, believe you have the power to repair."[8] Nachman's insight is startling. The ability to transgress and the ability to repent arise from the same source; we cannot have the one without the other. We all know for a fact that we have the ability to ruin our lives. How, then, can we doubt that our creative powers are as strong as our destructive ones? Anything that we can tear down we can also rebuild.

But this sort of faith requires a trust in possibilities that we may not have experienced firsthand. The knowledge of how I erred is very real, but the knowledge that I have the ability to repair my mistakes may be purely theoretical. And this is where most of us need to rely on the experience of others. Friends or mentors who share their own experiences of moral rehabilitation can give us a model to rely on. Possibilities that we can't imagine in our own lives may be easier to see in the lives of others. In this way, the possibility of our *teshuvah* relies on the fact of someone else's. Our faith is built, as it were, with spiritual capital that we borrow from others.

Hope is the spiritual foundation of *teshuvah*. But this doesn't mean that our faith in the possibility of renewal must be rock solid before we can begin rebuilding our lives. Sometimes just a ray of hope is enough to convince us that *teshuvah* is possible, and that, in turn, enables us to take small steps along the path of repentance. Those steps—an apology to someone whose feelings we hurt, a decision to try to break free from dysfunctional patterns of behavior—then reinforce our faith. Faith is not an all-or-nothing proposition. Rather, it grows gradually and often unevenly as we proceed along the path of *teshuvah*. The important thing is just that we have enough hope to believe that starting down that path is both possible and worthwhile.

36

Turning Faults into Merits

Resh Lakish said, "Great is repentance, for it
reduces one's deliberate sins to mere errors." But
did not Resh Lakish say at another time, "Great is
penitence, for it transforms one's deliberate sins
into merits"? There is no difficulty here: the latter
statement refers to penitence out of love; the former, to penitence out of fear.

Babylonian Talmud, *Yoma* 86b

In general, we think of repentance as a way of achieving expiation for the wrongs we have done. But Resh Lakish's teaching points us in a new and surprising direction. Repentance, he
suggests, can transform deliberate sins into merely inadvertent
ones. More surprising yet is the second teaching attributed to
him, according to which repentance turns deliberate sins into
merits! How are we to make sense of these apparently illogical
claims?

We judge deliberate misconduct more harshly than unintentional wrongs, and for good reason. Evil intent compounds the
wrong, for we have to confront not only the inappropriateness of
the deed (that someone endangered another's life or damaged
someone else's property), but also the maliciousness of that person's desires. Intent sometimes constitutes a separate offense, as
we know from cases of "thought crimes," such as conspiracy to
overthrow the government, which are illegal even if they are
never successfully carried out. So harmful intent can be an
offense in its own right, no less than a harmful act.

153

In this light it is easier to see what Resh Lakish is trying to say. To repent is, in part, to come to regret having committed a particular transgression. It is also to form the intention not to make the same mistake again. Through repentance, then, we disown our former evil intention and replace it with the intention to do good. In this way, Resh Lakish says, we can retroactively transform what we have done. The deed itself cannot be undone, but the misguided intent, the original desire to harm another, can be disclaimed. As a result, the malicious deed, by virtue of repentance, has been "downgraded" to an action that was wrong, but lacking in evil intent. The new intention, born of *teshuvah*, has negated the former one.

But how can this logic explain the still more radical view of Resh Lakish? Here I think the focus is not on changing the past, but on defining a new direction for the future. For *teshuvah*, after all, is ultimately about changing ourselves, not only clearing our record of past deeds that we are now ashamed of. Through the process of *teshuvah* we evolve morally, becoming the sort of people who can no longer conceive of falling back into the old patterns of misconduct that characterized our past. But how did this transformation occur if not through the examination of that very misconduct? Transgressions can become the springboard for tremendous moral growth, if only we do the hard work of *teshuvah* that enables us to learn from our mistakes.

In this way, repentance enables us to turn our moral liabilities into assets. Rabbi Soloveitchik captures the spiritual dynamic of this process:

> The years of sin are transformed into powerful impulsive forces which propel the sinner toward God. Sin is not to be forgotten, blotted out or cast into the depths of the sea. On the contrary, sin has to be remembered. It is the memory of sin that released the power within the inner depths of the soul of the penitent to do greater things than ever before. The energy of sin can be used to bring one to new heights.[9]

It would be preposterous if an accountant suggested that a debit was really a credit. But what is impossible on a financial balance sheet is eminently doable in the context of soul reckoning. Indeed, it is the very goal of *teshuvah* to transform the sins of the past into the roots of a new life. In a profound sense, then, repentance does turn our vices into virtues.

I have discussed the distinction between "repentance of fear" and "repentance of love" earlier in chapter 27. There the point was that the fear of punishment is sufficient to make us want to disown our past mistakes. But only the genuine desire to become better enables us to see our past failings as opportunities to build a new, purer life. When we love God and goodness, we are motivated to repent so thoroughly that our former transgressions really take on a positive cast, for they bring us to new heights.

Rabbi Kook, in characteristically mystical language, takes this idea to a new level. There is some goodness that resides within the evil that we do, and when we recognize this and, through *teshuvah*, release it, that goodness bursts forth and finds expression in a new life. He writes:

> One's perspective is enlarged through penitence.... All that seemed deficient, all that seemed ugly in the past, turns out to be full of majesty and grandeur as a phase of the greatness achieved through the progress of penitence.... Moreover, it is necessary to identify the good that is embodied in the depth of evil and to strengthen it—with the very force wherewith one recoils from evil. Thus will penitence serve as a force for good that literally transforms all the wrongdoings into virtues.[10]

The moral life of the penitent grows out of the ashes of the old life of transgressions, so those ashes are, in a sense, the fertilizer of a new righteous life. The past is no longer something to be regretted or disowned, but to be embraced for the possibilities contained within it.

Adin Steinsaltz, the contemporary Israeli Talmudic scholar and religious thinker, expresses this same idea somewhat more prosaically, though no less powerfully: "You should regard the faults as something constructive, like the beginning of a new and beautiful story."[11] Viewed from that perspective, our faults have indeed become our merits, a feat made possible only through the extraordinary transformative power of *teshuvah*.

Part VI

Teshuvah: Its Problems and Limits

37

Sinning Against Repentance

One who says, "I will sin and repent, sin and
repent"—
they give him no chance to do repentance.

Mishnah, Yoma **8:9**

The power of atonement is precisely that it offers transgressors the possibility of clearing the slate, reclaiming their good name. What was done can be undone. The past can be redeemed and, as it were, made to disappear. But this very idea—that transgressions can be wiped away—is potentially dangerous, for it threatens to undermine a key principle of justice: moral accountability. If *teshuvah* lets me off the hook for my misdeeds, how will I also be held accountable for them? If I know that expiation is available to me, no matter what I do wrong, why not continue in my hurtful ways? The more we acknowledge the power of *teshuvah*, the less the gravity of our sins seems to matter.

The Rabbis recognized this problem, and in this text they address it directly. *Teshuvah*, they tell us, cannot be abused. It is not a crutch on which we can rely as we continue to engage in inappropriate behavior. The temptation is to think of *teshuvah* as an escape clause from moral responsibility, as a "get-out-of-jail-free card" that we can use at any time. But this is to misconstrue the nature of *teshuvah*, which does not magically or automatically undo what we have done.

There are two ways of reading the message of this text. The wording "they give him no chance to do repentance" is probably better rendered in the passive: "he has no chance to do repentance."

This might mean simply that God will not receive such phony repentance, and so it is null and void. Such a person does not earn the release that comes with genuine repentance. For what enables us to atone for our mistakes is *genuine* repentance; no mere show of remorse or pro forma apology will suffice. The world is so construed that we cannot "game" the system of repentance. In this connection, it is worth considering the following Islamic teaching: "He who begs God's forgiveness for a sin but still persists in it is like one who mocks his Lord."[1] The Rabbis made the same point in a more graphic way:

> One who sins and confesses and yet does not repent—to what may such a person be compared? To one who holds a reptile [which renders him impure] such that even immersing in all the waters in the world will not purify him. But let him cast away the reptile and immerse in just forty *seahs* of water [the amount necessary for a *mikveh,* a pool for ritual purification], he will immediately be purified.
>
> **(Babylonian Talmud, Ta'anit 16a)**

Alternatively, the Sages might have been making a psychological observation. The person who imagines that she can continue to sin while relying on the option of repentance is never really capable of repentance. Such a person understands neither the nature of sin nor of repentance. Sin has a habitual quality to it. When we underestimate the power of the evil inclination within us or our ability to resist it, we come to think of transgression as a trivial matter. And similarly, we come to think of *teshuvah* as cheap and easily achieved. To adopt this attitude is to be trapped in a mindset that is precisely antithetical to the outlook needed for repentance. The point, then, is not that this person's repentance is unacceptable, but rather that such a person has no clue what repentance really is. For such a person, *teshuvah* remains a theoretical possibility, but a practical impossibility.

Interestingly, the passage cited above goes on to say, "[One who says,] 'I will sin and the Day of Atonement will atone'—the Day of Atonement does not atone." This is a surprising claim, given those biblical passages suggesting that Yom Kippur itself has the power to cleanse people of sin entirely: "For on that day He will atone for you to purify you from all your transgressions; before the LORD you shall be purified" (Leviticus 16:30). But the Rabbis want to say that the day itself does not effect atonement, at least not for those who imagine that this provides a license for immoral conduct.

There is no quick and easy way to redemption. Sin is not so trivial nor repentance so effortless. The opportunity that God gives us to be freed from the guilt and shame of our past is no backstage door through which we can escape unnoticed or unscathed. The Day of Atonement and *teshuvah* both require the hard work of soul reckoning and genuine self-transformation. The person who thinks otherwise imagines that the goal is simply to be magically cleansed of wrongdoing. But the real goal is radical transformation, the sort of reorientation of our lives that can happen only when we deeply appreciate the roots of our misdeeds and the difficult and painstaking work entailed in renewing our moral selves.

38

Jonah, Justice, and Repentance

The people of Nineveh believed God, so they
   called a fast
and put on sackcloth, from the greatest to the
   least of them ...
and they cried mightily unto God, and each person
turned from his evil ways, and from the violence
   of their hands.

Jonah 3:5, 3:8

The book of Jonah is traditionally read on the afternoon of Yom Kippur. At first blush, it's an odd choice. The book features a prophet who doesn't behave remotely the way prophets are supposed to behave; it includes the fantastical story of Jonah being swallowed by a whale; and the book's only penitents are the people of Nineveh, who were sworn enemies of the Israelites. Not exactly an inspiring tale for the holiest day of the year.

Jonah himself is surely among the most puzzling characters in the Bible. When God commissions him to go to Nineveh and call the inhabitants to repent, he runs in the opposite direction, jumps a ship, retreats into the recesses of the vessel, and falls asleep. After his ordeal in the belly of the fish, Jonah does go to Nineveh and tell them to repent. But when they do, Jonah is completely distraught and pleads with God to take his life. How can we make sense of Jonah's strange behavior? What motivates him? And especially, why is he so reluctant to help the Ninevites repent?

Although the story is certainly open to many interpretations, I suspect that Jonah is committed to justice and is rightfully concerned that repentance undermines just retribution.[2] The Ninevites have sinned and should pay for their transgressions. Why should God let them off the hook? And why should Jonah allow himself to be used as a vehicle for obstructing justice? The text gives us a sense that this is Jonah's view when he responds to God's forgiveness of the Ninevites:

> But it displeased Jonah exceedingly, and he was vexed. And he prayed to the LORD and said, "I pray Thee, O LORD, was not this my saying when I was still in my own country? Therefore I fled earlier to Tarshish, for I knew that You are a gracious God, and merciful, slow to anger and great in love, and repent of evil. Therefore now, O LORD, take my life from me, I pray You, for it is better for me to die than to live."
>
> (Johan 4:1–3)

Jonah plainly doesn't approve of God's decision to forgive the Ninevites in response to their repentance. Better that God should punish them for their sins. Perhaps Jonah feels this way about all sinners, or perhaps he only wants God to be strict with the Ninevites because they are Israel's enemies. We can't be sure. But what does seem clear is that Jonah would rather flee from God than be an instrument of God's compassion and, once forced into that role, would rather die than live.

The story testifies eloquently to the power of *teshuvah*, and also to its dangers. What if sinners can be forgiven and saved just by doing *teshuvah*? Don't their victims have the right to see them pay for their crimes? Justice appears to demand precisely what *teshuvah* short-circuits, the punishment of the offender.

All of us at times feel like Jonah. We want those who have harmed us to be tried, convicted, and punished, if not in an actual court of law, at least in the court of public opinion. No doubt that is why a victim's family members almost universally express satisfaction when the criminal is convicted and sentenced. At last, justice has been done; the wrong has been avenged. How awful it would be to have to tell the guilty party that he could avoid punishment if he would just repent of his crime. Jonah's message is an affront to justice. But then, so too is God's.[3]

In the closing verses of the book, God attempts to teach Jonah a lesson about compassion through the short-lived gourd that protects Jonah from the blazing sun. Jonah is pleased when God provides the gourd for his comfort and is distraught when God kills it.

> Then the Lord said, "You are concerned about the gourd, for which you have not labored and which you did not rear, which came up in a night and perished in a night. And should I then not be concerned for Nineveh, that great city, in which are more than one hundred and twenty thousand persons that cannot discern between their right hand and their left, and also much cattle?"
>
> **(Johah 4:10–11)**

Jonah counts on God's compassion to protect him from the heat of the sun but is offended when that same compassion is shown to his enemies, the Ninevites. But strict justice is not the order of the world, not for plants and certainly not for people. God is moved by the sincere penitence of the Ninevites, who respond immediately to Jonah's announcement and even go so far as to dress their cattle in sackcloth (3:8). Strict justice can be set aside. In the words of another prophet, "I [God] do not desire the death of the wicked, but rather that the wicked turn from his way and live" (Ezekiel 33:11).

Teshuvah evokes God's compassion and forgiveness. What makes the book of Jonah ironic—deliciously so—is that the Ninevites understand the value of repentance, while Jonah, the Israelite prophet, is clueless. Jonah wants a God who will execute justice, but God won't oblige. Jonah would prefer that *teshuvah* were not possible or, at least, not efficacious. But despite Jonah's best efforts, God's compassion toward penitents is undeterred. Repentance supersedes justice.

It is a message perfectly suited to the Day of Atonement. If justice prevails in the world, we're all lost. But the example of the Ninevites gives us hope that our fasting and turning from evil will reach God, who will show us compassion after all. Jonah is an object lesson for all who imagine (or even wish) that the world were governed by strict justice. The Ninevites among us know better, which gives them and us the confidence that *teshuvah* can change the course of history, right our wrongs, and reconcile us with God.

39

Irredeemable Sinners

Twenty-four things inhibit *teshuvah*....

Maimonides, *Mishneh Torah*, Laws of Repentance 4:1

Is repentance always an option? Are there transgressions so grievous that no possibility of *teshuvah* exists for them? Most of us intuitively sense that this must be so. Mass murderers, for example, must be beyond redemption. Their sin is so great that it is hard for most of us to imagine that there is any way for them to make up for their atrocities. Indeed, for some the very suggestion that this could be so is profoundly offensive.

Judaism has long reflected on this problem, which is really the problem of the limits of *teshuvah*. Just how powerful is *teshuvah*? Can it overcome even the most horrific crimes, the most hardened criminal? These questions bring us to the heart of the matter: how deeply engrained can sin be, and how effective can repentance be in redeeming the most egregious sinner?

Classical sources offer us several variations on this problem, but we will focus here on Maimonides' enumeration of these "impediments" to *teshuvah*. He categorizes these in the following ways:

(I) Sins so great that God does not give the sinner the opportunity to repent:

a) Leading others to commit transgressions (or preventing them from performing commandments)

b) Diverting someone from a good path to an evil one

c) Failing to dissuade someone from doing evil when it is in your power to do so

d) Saying, "I will sin and repent, sin and repent"

The central feature of these transgressions seems to be a failure on the part of these sinners to take responsibility for sins, either their own or those of others. Because the first step in *teshuvah* is to take responsibility for wrongdoing, these sinners cannot even get to first base, as it were. Whether they actively lead others to transgress or fail to prevent them from doing so, they have blurred the line between good and evil at a fundamental level. They regard evil as good or (just as problematic) insignificant, which is precisely the problem of those who think that they can just sin and then repent and clear their records. If you fail to recognize that sin is both serious and avoidable, then there is no possibility of repenting for it.

(II) Sins that create obstacles to *teshuvah*:

e) Separating yourself from the community

f) Deviating from Rabbinic consensus

g) Despising the commandments

h) Mocking your teachers

i) Hating (and so resisting) reproof

Here Maimonides turns his attention to obstacles of a different sort. Those who cut themselves off from the wisdom and guidance that facilitate *teshuvah* simply don't have the resources at their disposal to repent. It is self-evident to most Jewish authorities that the support of our teachers (both present and from ages past) and the connection to a community that provides spiritual support (but that also admonishes those who lose their way) are essential to penitents. Those who spurn the very guidance that prompts repentance have placed obstacles in their own way and find themselves unable to repent.

(III) Sins whose victims cannot be identified:

j) Cursing a multitude of people (rather than discrete individuals)

k) Taking stolen property

l) Taking lost property without attempting to locate its rightful owner

m) Taking the ox [that is, the property] of the poor (who are not well known and who migrate from place to place)

n) Taking a bribe to pervert justice

The problems here are logistical in that the penitents cannot locate all the victims of their transgressions. Because making amends to the injured party is an essential component of complete *teshuvah*, these sorts of offenses, by their nature, are not amenable to atonement.

(IV) Sins that are regarded lightly and imagined to be permissible:

o) Eating a meal at someone's table when there isn't sufficient food for the master of the house, because this is akin to theft

p) Using something that the poor have given as a pledge

q) Looking at someone who is sexually forbidden (for example, a close relative or someone married to another)

r) Exalting yourself at the expense of another

s) Sowing suspicion about those who are upright

Lots of activities that we know aren't exactly acceptable are also difficult to identify as sins. They may strike us as technically wrong, but trivial, and so we think, "What's the harm in that?" Precisely because it is so easy to overlook the hurt we cause others in these cases, they don't even make it onto the list of things we feel we need to repent for.

(V) Sins that readily become habitual:

t) Gossip

u) Slander

v) Being quick tempered

w) Harboring evil thoughts

x) Associating with evildoers

Certain sins have a kind of gravitational pull about them. Once we begin to engage in them, it is very difficult to extricate ourselves from the habit. Some of these are activities that we are psychologically inclined toward—speaking or thinking ill of others, for example. For many of us, they just seem to come naturally. Associating with the wrong crowd, on the other hand, may not come naturally, but social bonds once established are difficult to sever.

We might want to categorize these impediments somewhat differently than Maimonides did. Some barriers to *teshuvah* are *psychological*—we tend to minimize the significance of small misdeeds or underestimate how easily we become habituated to wrongdoing. *Teshuvah*, as we know, requires a very highly developed sense of our own weak spots and regular vigilance about the ways in which we can resist temptation. Other barriers to *teshuvah* are more *moral*. These involve a lack of moral insight, a failure to properly distinguish right from wrong behaviors. Finally, there are *practical* barriers in some cases. These are the times when our behavior has far-reaching consequences that cannot readily be identified, isolated, and atoned for.

What is most striking about this list of obstacles to *teshuvah*, however, is the absence of specific sins that are especially gruesome or morally repugnant—child molestation, torture, or mass murder. To be sure, some of these could fall under the category of sins whose victims cannot be identified. But on the whole, Maimonides appears less concerned with the scale of the sin committed than with the dynamics of *teshuvah* itself and the ways in which certain transgressions create roadblocks in the process.

Perhaps most striking of all, Maimonides concludes this lengthy enumeration with a disclaimer:

> All these and similar things, even though they impair *teshuvah*, do not prevent it. Rather, if a person does *teshuvah* for them, he is certainly a penitent and he has a share in the world to come.
>
> **(*Mishneh Torah*, Laws of Repentance 4:6)**

After explaining how some behaviors make repentance well-nigh impossible, he now wants us to believe that the door to *teshuvah* is open nonetheless. How are we to understand this about-face?

I suggest that Maimonides, and Jewish tradition as a whole, walks a fine line between the reality that some behaviors are antithetical to *teshuvah* and the belief that renewal is an ever-present possibility. To focus exclusively on the former would discourage sinners from even beginning to do *teshuvah*; to focus exclusively on the latter would remove any incentive to avoid sins in the first place. Thus, no matter how great our sins, Judaism teaches that *teshuvah* is still possible. But, lest we come to think of *teshuvah* as some sort of cosmic guarantee that we can sin with impunity, Judaism reinforces the message that certain sins so obstruct the path, or diminish the incentive to follow it, that they make *teshuvah* practically impossible.

40

A Hardened Heart

But the LORD hardened Pharaoh's heart, so he
would not let the children of Israel go.

Exodus 10:20

There may be no more disturbing passage in all of the Torah
than this, that God purposefully made Pharaoh obstinate in
order to punish him and make an object lesson of him. What sort
of God is this? Surely we face many obstacles in doing *teshuvah*,
but God should not be one of them! And the matter is only made
worse by the fact that this point is repeated as many as a dozen
times throughout the Exodus narrative.

The Rabbis were likewise troubled by this idea and sought to
explain it in a midrash:

> "For I have hardened his heart" (Exodus 10:1). Rabbi Yohanan
> said: Does this not provide heretics with ground for arguing
> that he had no means of repenting, since it says: "For I have
> hardened his heart"? To which Rabbi Simeon ben Lakish
> replied: Let the mouths of the heretics be stopped up. "Surely
> God will scorn the scorners" (Proverbs 3:34). When God
> warns a person once, twice, and even a third time, and he still
> does not repent, then does God close his heart against repen-
> tance so that He should exact vengeance from him for his sins.
> Thus it was with the wicked Pharaoh.
>
> **(Exodus Rabbah 13:3; also Exodus Rabbah 11:6)**

For most of us, this will hardly seem like a satisfying explanation.
In the first place, this contradicts other, far more compassionate

views of God. Ezekiel says of God, "I have no pleasure in the death of the wicked, but that the wicked turn from his way and live" (Ezekiel 33:11). Any God who closes off the possibility of repentance just to exact punishment from us is a God most of us would not want to worship.

The underlying point, though, may not be so difficult for us to accept when we consider it more closely. We cannot permit repentance to be an easy way to escape the consequences of our deeds. In fact, we are rightly skeptical of a hardened criminal who repents precisely in order to avoid punishment. In our day, we would surely be inclined to dismiss any claims of repentance by Nazi war criminals, for instance, no matter how much they insisted on their sincerity. Repentance cannot be allowed to undermine the demands of justice, which include the demand that people must pay the price for their crimes. In the view of some Rabbis, then, the opportunity for repentance is limited and must be balanced with the need for just punishment.[4] In theological terms, God wants us to repent and gives us plenty of opportunities to do so, but even God's patience is not infinite.[5]

Contemporary readers who find even this theological view objectionable may be drawn to an interpretation that minimizes any supernatural intervention in the story altogether. God doesn't intervene in history to harden people's hearts. Rather, there is a natural, psychological progression whereby people who transgress repeatedly become more and more set in their ways. The path of repentance closes to them because they can no longer find it or simply no longer care to look. In this sense, a "hardened heart" is indeed a significant obstacle to repentance, but it is an obstacle that arises naturally from a pattern of misdeeds. Perhaps God has so created us that we have the power to become our own worst enemies in just this way.[6] Perhaps this is to ensure that we ultimately confront the natural consequences of our deeds, which can then be understood as punishments.

The ultimate message about hardening our hearts, then, is that we must take great care in how we channel our passions, or direct our hearts. It is often noted that for the ancient Israelites the heart was the seat of emotion and moral decision.[7] It is less frequently noted that the expression most often used in connection with Pharaoh's hardened heart is *chazak lev,* literally, "to strengthen one's heart" (e.g., Exodus 10:20). In his case, the "strengthening" was in the direction of arrogance and obstinacy. But we could strengthen our hearts in other ways, as well. This is the concluding message of Psalm 27, which employs the very same language as that of Pharaoh's heart: "Hope in the LORD; be strong, let your heart take courage, and hope in the LORD" (v. 14). The psalmist encourages us to strengthen our hearts in a way that causes us to trust God's benevolence and that heightens our yearning to live always in the shelter of God's presence (v. 4). This sort of resolve is precisely the sort of "strengthening of heart" that enables us to counteract our natural tendencies to become hardened to our own transgressions. Perhaps this is why this psalm has traditionally been recited throughout the month of Elul and during the High Holy Days. Just when our attention is directed toward our need for repentance, we pray for the sort of hardened/strengthened heart that will enable us to persist in the work of *teshuvah.*

41

Repenting to the Dead

The one who sins against a person who dies
before one can ask forgiveness should bring a
minyan [ten adult members of the community] to
that person's grave and say in their presence, "I
have sinned against Adonai the God of Israel and
against this person. I did thus and so." If the individual were obligated to pay money to the
deceased, that person should pay that money to
that person's heirs. If the individual does not
know who the heirs are, the individual should
leave that money with the court and confess.

Maimonides, *Mishneh Torah*, Laws of Repentance 2:11

It would be reasonable to suppose that if someone dies before
we can seek his forgiveness, the obligation to do so simply goes
away. Just as the harm that we caused dies with him, so too does
our need to do *teshuvah*. How, then, do we make sense of this
teaching? How can we confess our wrongs to the dead, and moreover, why should we need to?

The answer to this question may be hinted at in the provi-
sion that the sinner should bring a *minyan* of people to the grave
to witness the confession. The quorum of ten adults necessary for
public worship, a *minyan* is the smallest number of people who
together constitute a Jewish community. To call together a *minyan*, then, is symbolically to assemble the community. In this case,
they will hear the confession that the deceased can no longer
receive. In essence, the sinner, no longer able to confess to the

173

individual he wronged, must instead confess to the entire community, in microcosm.

The implicit message is that each time we harm another person, we damage the community as a whole. So although this particular individual has died, the community of which she was a part has not, and the community needs to receive the confession in order to heal the rift that this behavior has caused. Bringing the *minyan* to the graveside only reinforces the fact that they are present as surrogates for the deceased. It is hard to imagine a more powerful illustration of the biblical concept that the deceased is "gathered to his people." Indeed, the one who died is now absorbed into her community, and so their presence is, in essence, synonymous with that of the deceased.

This teaching is extended in connection with the need to pay restitution. Any money owed to the deceased needs to be paid to her heirs, if they can be located. But if they cannot, the debt is not simply canceled. Rather, it goes to the court, which, once again, represents the repository for the needs of the community. What we owe to the dead, we owe to the community of which she was a part.

For some years I participated in a synagogue-based *chevrah kadisha*, a traditional Jewish burial society. We were a group of volunteers who cared for deceased members of the congregation, washing the bodies, performing the ritual purification (*taharah*), and clothing them in shrouds before we placed them gently in the coffin. It was a somber and sacred task, one performed in virtual silence and with utmost respect for the dignity of the deceased. But for me the most moving moment in the entire ritual came at the very conclusion, when we gathered around the coffin and the leader of the group would address the deceased man by name and say, "We apologize for any indignity that we may have inadvertently caused you in the process of this *taharah*." We are capable of offending others even after they have died, and we are no less obliged to offer our apology on account of that fact.

On the psychological level, there is very likely another value involved in this rather striking practice. Many of us know the experience of feeling guilty toward those who have died—parents we neglected, friends we let down, acquaintances we mistreated.

When they die (especially if they die with little advance warning), we can be left with much unfinished business and a painful feeling that we have missed the opportunity ever to make amends. Some might attempt to relieve this guilt by writing a letter or confessing to a friend or family member of the deceased. The alternative of living indefinitely with the unrelieved guilt is sometimes simply not bearable.

I admit that I have never heard of anyone who has actually engaged in this ritual of confession at the grave of the deceased. Most of us would probably find the idea bizarre. But this teaching confirms what we know to be true on an emotional level, that the need to apologize does not in fact die with the people we have injured. Even if they are at peace, often we are not. And so the practice of confessing directly to the dead offers us a way to clear our conscience.

Sometimes, though, confession and apology are not sufficient. The desire to do *teshuvah* frequently includes the need to repair the damage we have caused—by making monetary restitution, as this ruling suggests, but also by comforting those we have emotionally hurt or honoring those we have demeaned. And what shall we do if those individuals are dead or, what amounts to the same thing, unavailable? We may have used a racial slur against a certain individual who was a stranger to us, and we now have no way to find her and make our amends. In such cases, there is no grave to go to, and moreover, the verbal confession alone would fall short of what we feel we need to do in order to make up for our mistake.

The Rabbis identify such cases as times when *teshuvah* is not possible. But there may be another way, one suggested by philosopher Martin Buber in one of the few places where he addressed issues of *teshuvah*. He wrote, "The wounds of the order-of-being can be healed in infinitely many other places than those at which they were inflicted."[8] If we have insulted a particular disabled person whom we can no longer find, we can give our support to organizations that work to protect their rights. If years ago we turned our backs on someone in an hour of need and we can no longer find that person, we can give extra care to those around us now when they come to us for help. The opportunities for doing *teshuvah* are not limited just because the particular person we harmed cannot be contacted. The work of repair can go on, with other people in other places. The fabric of our world can be made whole in one place, even if our actions rent it in another.

The need to do *teshuvah* transcends death. Fortunately, so too do the opportunities to do so.

Part VII

Teshuvah: Its Moral and Spiritual Meaning

42

Overcoming Guilt

Repentance, at least in its perfect form, genuinely
annihilates the psychic quality called "guilt." And
so it bursts the chain of evil's reproductive power
which is transmitted through the growth in evil
of men and times. This then is the way in which
it enables men to embark on new and guiltless
courses.

Max Scheler[1]

Guilt is paradoxically both a prerequisite to repentance and an
impediment to it. On the one hand, to feel guilty is to feel bad
about our transgressions, which is a critical step in the process of
teshuvah. On the other hand, to feel guilty is to feel unworthy,
ashamed, and so incapable of extricating ourselves from our
transgressions and its effects, both on ourselves and on others. In
truth, *teshuvah* both builds upon and transforms the experience of
guilt in ways that point toward its revolutionary nature in the life
of penitents.

Think about the many distinct ways in which the word
"guilt" is used in connection with the moral life. Guilt is sometimes an objective judgment on a person's behavior, as when a
jury pronounces the defendant "guilty, as charged." Guilt is sometimes simply the internal awareness of being culpable for doing
something wrong. In this sense, it is an expression of conscience.
As a feeling, guilt is susceptible to many variations and arises in
various circumstances. I can feel guilty for a particular thing I
have done or for being a certain kind of person without reference

179

to specific misdeeds. I can feel guilty for things I haven't personally done at all, as when I have benefitted from the misdeeds of others or when someone in my community commits a transgression and I feel "guilty by association." And, of course, like all emotions, guilt can be experienced more or less intensely, depending on the gravity of our actions and even on the extent to which we have fine-tuned our sensitivity to our smallest misdeeds.[2]

Some have tried to distinguish between feeling guilty for what we have done and feeling guilty for who we are. Those who draw this distinction often suggest that the former is (or, at least, can be) a very useful feeling, while the second is potentially debilitating. But this distinction is probably too facile. Our deeds are, after all, a reflection of our selves and the best window into our moral character. Moreover, feeling bad about ourselves is sometimes precisely what motivates us to begin the difficult work of repentance, as any addict who has "hit bottom" can attest. It is not so easy, then, to distinguish "good guilt" from "bad guilt."

It is more helpful, I think, to begin by acknowledging that feeling guilty is an essential component of moral development. We cannot grow as moral people if we do not feel some guilt at appropriate times in response to our behavior, our attitudes, and our character defects. In this sense, guilt is the engine that can, if properly channeled, propel us down the path of repentance. Absent feelings of guilt, we would lack either the awareness of our wrongdoing or the requisite discomfort about it to motivate us to change. Guilt is the emotional component of self-judgment, and such self-evaluation is essential to repentance.

But guilt is also the experience of feeling burdened by our transgressions, the sense that they are so numerous, grievous, or deeply engrained that they are inescapable. Guilt in this sense undercuts hope, for it is experienced as a judgment not only on the past, but on the future, as well. This is the sense of guilt that finds expression in Psalm 38:4–5:

> There is no soundness in my flesh because of Your rage,
> no wholeness in my bones because of my sin.
> For my iniquities have overwhelmed me;
> they are like a heavy burden, more than I can bear.

The experience of repentance emerges in the space between these two experiences of guilt. Repentance builds upon the experience of responsibility for our transgressions and the remorse that turns this responsibility from an abstract realization into a concrete call to action. But then repentance, once begun, relieves the burden of sin in the life of the penitent. The awareness of transgression remains, but the weight of it is lessened, so that the penitent now feels a paradoxical awareness of guilt and freedom from it. The philosopher Max Scheler associated this shift with a stage of repentance that moves beyond the focus on specific deeds to one that attends to the whole person:

> The more Repentance ceases to be mere repentance of conduct and becomes repentance of Being, the more it grasps the *root* of guilt perceived, to pluck it out of the Person and restore the latter's freedom.[3]

This is the promise of repentance, that it accentuates the experience of guilt, but in the service of freedom, not servitude. Guilt is no longer just the impetus to repent, the sort of experience that initiates the process but then is quickly left behind. Rather, guilt becomes a trusted companion on the path of repentance, for its appearance is a marker of work that remains to be done, work that the penitent undertakes joyfully. Guilt in this way is robbed of its heaviness. It can be borne lightly, which is not to say effortlessly. For guilt remains what it has always been: an awareness of failing, of missing the mark, of incompleteness. But *teshuvah* enables us to transcend guilt, to turn it from something that darkens our path into a light that illuminates it.

43

As God Sees Us

The examination of conscience is thus justified;
my own observation of myself is the attempt of
self-awareness to approximate the absolute view;
I desire to know myself as I am known.

Paul Ricoeur[4]

One way to understand the goal of soul reckoning is to think of it in terms of perspective. Most of us live our lives much of the time without a genuine perspective on who we are. Some of us walk around with a highly inflated idea of ourselves. We see ourselves as special, entitled to privileges that others don't enjoy. We carry ourselves with a certain haughtiness that is palpable in our encounters with others. We talk about ourselves excessively, especially our accomplishments or status or connections to other, highly important people. We crave being the center of attention, and even when we are, we are never quite satisfied. Some of us are led into transgression because we have convinced ourselves that the ordinary rules don't apply to people like us. We delude ourselves into thinking that we are "above the law," and for just that reason, we run afoul of it.

Others of us are deeply insecure and suffer from perennially low self-esteem. We are endlessly self-denigrating, telling others that what we say or do is really unimportant. We may associate with people we look up to, even idolize, so that we can feel better about ourselves vicariously. All too often, though, this strategy backfires, for this only feeds our comparisons of ourselves with others and deepens our sense of unworthiness. In minimizing our own worth, we invite others to pity us, and when we sense that we have evoked that pity, we feel reaffirmed in our self-perception. Some of us hold ourselves in such low esteem that we don't believe we are capable of living up to the standards that other, ordinary people live up to. We use our lack of self-esteem as an excuse to explain our misdeeds, which in turn make us feel worse about ourselves and so more prone to do what we know we shouldn't.

In truth, these two groups of people, though they appear to be opposites, are one and the same. Arrogant people are very insecure and lonely, and they expect attention and deference precisely to mask their deep-seated sense of inadequacy. The overblown image of themselves that they project is the converse of the low self-esteem in which they hold themselves. Such people suffer from the need to fill a deep hole in their psyches that seems never to be filled. The more that others treat them as privileged, the more they feel entitled to bend the rules in their favor. And the more they do so, the worse they feel about themselves and the more urgent is the need to project even more exaggerated images of themselves. And so the cycle continues.

When we engage in *cheshbon hanefesh*, we attempt to break out of these dysfunctional cycles and put ourselves in proper perspective. Our goal is to see ourselves as we truly are. This means that we are neither as all-important or as pitiable as we may be inclined to think. Because if we fall into either of these traps, we cannot find that place of balance in which we both hold ourselves to high standards of moral behavior and also adopt a healthy, accepting attitude toward ourselves and our moral failings. In truth, we are all pretty much the same—flawed human beings who are capable in most cases of distinguishing right from wrong and who frequently struggle with our own tendency to make the wrong choice. We know deep down that we are subject to the same moral rules as everyone else, and we know that when we occasionally fail, we are able to hold ourselves accountable and begin a process of self-correction, of *teshuvah*.

In theological terms, the goal of gaining perspective on our lives can be put in terms of seeing ourselves as God would see us. God knows what we are made of. God knows where we stand in the order of creation. And the truth is that we are both "little lower than the angels" (Psalm 8:6) and "mere dust and ashes" (Genesis 18:27). In the words of the traditional morning service:

> What are we? What is our life? What is our goodness? What is our righteousness?... All the heroes are as nothing before Thee, and men of renown as though they never existed, the wise as if they were without knowledge, the intelligent as though they lacked understanding, for most of their doings are worthless and the days of their lives are vain in Your sight. Man is not far above beast, for all is vanity.
>
> However, we are Your people, Your people of the covenant, the children of Abraham, Your friend, to whom You made a promise on Mount Moriah.

This dual perspective—that we are exalted moral creatures who are in relationship with God and that we are frail, mortal creatures whose lives begin and end in nothingness—provides us with the proper frame for making sense of our lives and especially for continuing on the path of repentance. If we think too highly of ourselves, we will come to presume that we have no need of repentance. If we think too little of ourselves, we will come to believe that we are incapable of it. It is precisely when we see ourselves as God would see us, in the unsparing light of truth, that we know we are both in need of repentance and capable of it.

In just this way, *teshuvah* is about a commitment to truth. Not just the truth of acknowledging what we have really done, but perhaps hidden from others and even ourselves. That is simply the first step in soul reckoning: honest self-disclosure. But *teshuvah* requires a more far-reaching commitment to honesty and truthfulness, which is that we embrace the truth about our humanity, about the human condition, and about our true place in the world. Only then will we be able to hold ourselves accountable to the highest moral standards and also to believe that, despite our failings in the past, we can—indeed, must—strive to attain them.

44

Divine Freedom

> Penitence is the aspiration for the true original
> freedom, which is the divine freedom, wherein
> there is no enslavement of any kind.
>
> **Rabbi Abraham Isaac Kook[5]**

The goal of the penitent is to find true freedom—freedom from the mistakes of the past and from the compulsion to repeat them, freedom from shame, freedom from the shackles of self-deception, self-aggrandizement, and self-denigration. Freedom to live a life of wholeness and integrity, freedom to become the people we were created to be. But where can we find a model of such freedom? And lacking a model, how can we begin to create such a life?

The Torah provides such a model in the way it depicts God. This will strike many readers as odd. If God is perfect, how could God be a model of *teshuvah*, which implies a trajectory of making mistakes, learning from them, and improving?

Careful readers of the Torah know, however, that God is far from perfect. God destroys all of humanity (save Noah and his family) during the Flood, kills the Egyptian firstborn in order to "gain honor" (Exodus 14:4), orders Moses to annihilate the Amalekites and then Joshua to massacre the Canaanites, and so on. God makes decisions and later regrets them (see Genesis 6:6; Exodus 32:14). And, though the Torah never provides a straightforward account of God's moral development, the God we encounter in the Bible does change over time, often in ways that suggest a deepening compassion, first for the Israelites as a whole and later for the fate of the individual. God is free, it seems, to learn from the mistakes of the past and to refine this evolving relationship with humanity.[6]

But there are many even more important senses in which God is free. God is unencumbered by the need to share power with any other deity. God's dominion extends over all creation. And that is true temporally as well as spatially. God is unconstrained by the limits of physicality, sexual desire, or mortality. Moreover, God possesses unlimited abilities to appear both within and beyond the natural order—now in a lowly bush, then in a cloud of fire, yet later in a still, small voice. No doubt it is this absolute lack of form or constraint that is reflected in the Torah's struggle to resolve the question of God's name. For we can only name those things whose defining traits we can identify with certainty. But when Moses questions God at the burning bush about what to say when the Israelites press him to identify God by name, he gets only the most enigmatic of answers: *Ehyeh asher ehyeh*, "I am/will be what I am/will be" (Exodus 3:14). God refuses to be pinned down in terms that would inherently limit God's nature. Or, to put the point positively, God is by definition mysterious, beyond comprehension, infinite, and dynamic. God is the epitome of freedom.

The Torah, of course, admonishes us repeatedly to imitate God. "Be holy as I, the LORD your God, am holy" (Leviticus 19:2). The Rabbis elaborated on this theme frequently, as in the following midrash:

> As the ways of Heaven are to be gracious, graciously bestowing gifts not only upon those who know Him but also upon those who do not know Him, so you are to bestow gifts upon one another. And, as the ways of Heaven are to be long-suffering, long-suffering with the wicked and then accepting them in repentance, so you are to be long-suffering [with the wicked] for their good and not impatient to impose punishment upon them. For, as the ways of Heaven are abundant in lovingkindness, ever leaning to lovingkindness, so are you ever to lean toward doing kindness to others rather than lean toward doing them harm.
>
> (*Tanna de-ei Eliyahu*, 135)[7]

Texts like this prompt us to ask: if God, above all, is free, and if our task in life, above all, is to imitate God, what would it mean to imitate divine freedom?

I suggest that the answer to this question can be found in the path of repentance. For God's essential quality, as the story of the burning bush reminds us, is to be ever-changing. God is dynamic, always in the process of becoming, never static or definable. And that is precisely the quality—in the moral, rather than the metaphysical realm—that epitomizes the penitent, who is constantly striving to break free from the chains of the past, to become a new and better person. There is no room here for complacency or compromise with "what is." The goal, no matter how far short we fall, is to transform ourselves, and then to transform ourselves yet again. The experience of repentance is of being in a state of constant evolution, never at rest. There is infinite opportunity for improvement, and this realization keeps us always aware of our radical freedom. And this is true whether on any given day we succeed or fail in doing *teshuvah*, for either way we are aware that success and failure are both the result of choices freely made. To repent is to exercise our freedom to choose, day by day and hour by hour, the sort of people we will be.

All of us are like God, for we are created in God's image and have within us a spark of the Divine. But we are most like God when we realize our capacity for freedom, when we strike out on a new and unprecedented path in an effort to remake ourselves, all the more so when that path brings us into closer, more intimate relationship with God. When we do *teshuvah*, we make God's freedom our own.

45

Primordial *Teshuvah*

Six things preceded the creation of the world. Some were actually created, and others came up only in God's thought as what was to be created. Torah and the throne of glory were created. The creation of the fathers, Israel, the Temple, and the name of the Messiah came up only in God's thought. Rabbi Ahavah son of Rabbi Ze'era said: So, too repentance.

Genesis Rabbah 1:4[8]

What can it mean that repentance preceded the creation of the world? Surely before the creation of human beings, repentance would be pointless. Indeed, with no one yet to repent and nothing to repent for, it isn't even clear what repentance would mean in this context.

Although this teaching makes no chronological sense, it does point to a profound spiritual message. Long before sin entered the world, God had already prepared the antidote to it. At one level, this might be thought of as just a question of careful pre-planning on God's part. God wanted to provide the mechanism for overcoming transgressions even before any transgressions could be committed. Like the circus hands who spread out the safety net long before the acrobats begin their high-wire act, God anticipated the possibility (or certainty) that humans would be sinful and made sure that *teshuvah* would be available when it was needed. God was foresighted, as well as compassionate, we might conclude.

But I think the Rabbis were trying to say something about the nature of the world, and of *teshuvah*, more than about God's qualities of planfulness. In Rabbi Kook's elegant formulation:

> Penitence is present in the depths of existence because it was projected before the creation of the world, and before sin had occurred there had already been readied the repentance for it. Therefore, nothing is more certain than penitence, and in the end everything will be redressed and perfected.[9]

Teshuvah is built into the structure of the universe, like the laws of gravity or thermodynamics. The world that God created is a world in which redemption has been assured from the beginning. There is a moral structure to human life, not only in the sense that God purportedly rewards the righteous and punishes the wicked, but also in the sense that the struggle between good and evil in the world has a predetermined end. By putting *teshuvah* first in the order of creation, God made certain that goodness and redemption would prevail in the end. Everything that will ever happen in human history unfolds in the context of a world in which *teshuvah* is foundational. It is not just that humans need *teshuvah* to overcome their (future) transgressions; it is that human life as we know it is impossible without the assurance of *teshuvah*.

The implications of this for the nature of humankind are far reaching. What sort of creatures are we if we live in a world where *teshuvah* is endlessly available to us? Philosopher Adin Steinsaltz addresses this in his penetrating essay on repentance:

> Certain sages go so far as to include repentance among the entities created before the world itself. The implication of this remarkable statement is that repentance is a universal, primordial phenomenon; in such a context it has two meanings. One is that it is embedded in the root structure of the world; the other, that before man was created, he was given the possibility of changing the course of his life. In this latter sense repentance is the highest expression of man's capacity to choose freely—it is a manifestation of the Divine in man.[10]

The possibility of doing *teshuvah* represents radical freedom—freedom from the past, freedom even to alter the meaning of past events, to turn our faults into merits. Repentance is the most powerful force in human life, precisely because it enables us to remake ourselves into different sorts of creatures, to become morally and spiritually "new creations." This kind of freedom is a metaphysical force, something that defies the ordinary laws governing life on this planet, laws that preclude the possibility of moving backward in time or undoing what has already been done. *Teshuvah*, then, must precede creation, for it embodies a kind of freedom that could only exist outside the bounds of the created world.

When we do *teshuvah*, we participate in a kind of supernatural existence that connects us with God, who also is radically free. In just this sense, repentance entails a kind of *imitatio dei*. The more we engage in *teshuvah*, the freer we are, and the more we actualize that freedom, the more we are like God, who is perfectly free. From this perspective, the meaning of this teaching that *teshuvah* existed before creation is that it is the manifestation of divine freedom, the quality of God's that humankind is meant to emulate.

Teshuvah is a prerequisite for human life.[11] It was present before the beginning of time—assuring us that there is a path to redemption, enabling us to transcend in the moral realm the laws of causality that operate in the physical realm, providing us with the common ground for our freedom and God's. Because *teshuvah* was present before creation, the very structure of the world is conducive to the healing of our moral brokenness. Far more than the safety net that catches us when we fall, *teshuvah* is the divine force within us that makes us free and the assurance God has given us that our moral striving is not for naught.

46

Past and Future

For there is no repentance which does not from
its inception enclose the blueprint of a new heart.
Repentance kills only to create. It annihilates only
to rebuild. It is already building secretly where it
still seems to destroy.

Max Scheler[12]

Repentance is both end and beginning, the dying of old habits and the creation of a "new heart," the closing of one chapter of our lives and the start of another. But this shutting of one door and opening of another is not merely sequential, or even causal. The wonder of *teshuvah* is that it creates and destroys simultaneously, as part of a single process. In doing *teshuvah* we discover one of the essential truths of human life—that letting go of what was enables us to embrace that which is just emerging, which in turn helps us let go.

The personal transformation that repentance brings about requires nothing less than the death of one self and the birth of another. The person I was—the one who lost his temper, or lied, or was arrogant—must give way to a new person, who is temperate, truthful, and humble. But the transition between the two does not occur at some determinate point, like stepping across a threshold from one room into another. The transformation is more organic, like the process by which a moth becomes a butterfly. As we scrutinize ways of thinking and behaving that have not served us well, we begin to discover that there is a new way of being, and as that new possibility becomes progressively more real to us, the way we have lived in the past gradually fades away. The past dies and the future is born in one interactive process. As American poet T. S. Eliot wrote, "In my beginning is my end," and then, later in the same poem, "In my end is my beginning."[13]

I have witnessed these transformations up close among people in my twelve-step group dozens of times in recent years. Each person follows his own trajectory. Some spend years in limbo, talking about moving toward a life of greater sobriety and wholeness, but actually falling repeatedly back into old, dysfunctional patterns. Then, sometimes quite dramatically and unpredictably, a person finds the inner resources to break with his self-destructive behavior and the new self that emerges is the polar opposite of the person I had known for years. In other people this same process unfolds more gradually and steadily over a much longer period of time. But whether gradually or suddenly, the essence of the transformation is always the same: the person who was must give way to make room for someone new.

This is the magic, as it were, of *teshuvah*, which is no sleight of hand, but a genuine destructive/creative process that gives new life to souls that were moribund. How shall we understand this transformative process that is the essence of *teshuvah*? What is it, exactly, that enables the penitent to break radically with the past and embrace a future or, perhaps better, the possibility of a future that may be only a dream?

There is courage here, to be sure, and a strength of character that was hidden and now emerges from the shadows and asserts itself. It is the sort of strength that the Rabbis must surely have had in mind when they wrote, "Who is strong? The one who conquers his own inclination" (*Pirkei Avot* 4:1). But *teshuvah* also depends upon a kind of faith, the sort of faith that the New Testament defines as "the assurance of things hoped for, the conviction of things not seen" (Hebrews 11:1). At the point when a person comes to have faith that she can be renewed, the process of renewal is already at work, undermining the foundations of the past and laying the foundations for the future. In just this way, *teshuvah* is an irreducibly spiritual process, even for those who disavow any affinity for the spiritual life. For it entails a belief that I can both let go of the only way of being I have ever known and embrace a way of being that I am only now beginning to imagine. The leap into the unknown *is* the break with the past.

But this sort of faith is never easy or straightforward. It is effortful, and even the most successful penitents suffer setbacks, misgivings, and fear. Indeed, overcoming that fear is perhaps the single greatest challenge for those on the path of repentance. I know of no better description of this fear and the struggle to overcome it than this passage, taken from the Catholic theologian Henri Nouwen:

> You have an idea of what the new country looks like. Still, you are very much at home, although not truly at peace, in the old country. You know the ways of the old country, its joys and pains, its happy and sad moments. You have spent most of your days there. Even though you know that you have not found there what your heart most desires, you remain quite attached to it. It has become part of your very bones.
>
> Now you have come to realize that you must leave it and enter the new country, where your Beloved dwells. You know that what helped and guided you in the old country no longer works, but what else do you have to go by? You are being asked to trust that you will find what you need in the new country. That requires the death of what has become so precious to you: influence, success, yes, even affection and praise.
>
> Trust is so hard, since you have nothing to fall back on. Still, trust is what is essential. The new country is where you are called to go, and the only way to go there is naked and vulnerable.[14]

Trust or faith is what enables us first to believe that a new life is possible, then to imagine ourselves living with greater integrity, and finally to take one step at a time toward making that life a reality. And there is no faith without risks. We must venture into new territory, in Nouwen's powerful metaphor, and we cannot do so without feeling vulnerable. Destroying an old self and creating a new one requires nothing less.

Like water, *teshuvah* is both destructive and creative. It dissolves the person you were but simultaneously provides the moisture you need to grow anew. It erodes the hard edges of your willfulness but also refreshens your spirit. It can turn the tallest barriers of moral blindness into rubble while it also gently nourishes the hidden seeds of hope buried deep in your soul. *Teshuvah,* like water, has the power both to wash away past sin and to shower you with the blessing of a new future, if only you trust it and allow yourself to be carried along in its current.

47

Ahead of the Righteous

Rabbi Abbahu said, "In the place where penitents stand, even the wholly righteous cannot stand."
Babylonian Talmud, *Berakhot* **34b**

This is surely among the most puzzling statements on *teshuvah* in the classical sources. How can it be that the penitent is on a higher level than the wholly righteous person? Leaving aside the question of whether anyone could ever meet that description, surely a "wholly righteous" person, by definition, must be better than one who has sinned, even if that sin was followed by acts of repentance. After all, transgressors can never undo the past, and so their former life remains forever a part of their life story and their identity. Surely it is better never to have sinned at all than to have sinned and repented.[15] How could it be otherwise?

The Talmud provides no explanation for Abbahu's puzzling view, leaving ample room for speculation. We can begin to penetrate his thought if we abandon the seemingly self-evident idea that the fewer sins we have on our record, the better off we are. This quantitative perspective treats people like merchandise—we have greater value if we have fewer defects. But Abbahu apparently understands human life to be dynamic, where process is primary and the perfection of the product is secondary. Somehow there is a value in doing *teshuvah* that exceeds the value of a completely clean slate. But what is this?

Abbahu's point may be that we gain something through the process of repentance—a degree of self-awareness, an appreciation for human frailty, or a level of humility—that is valuable in its own right. When we look deeply into the causes of our misdeeds and apologize to those we have harmed, we emerge from that process with a richer sense of our own humanity. There is something noble, at once profoundly shattering and healing, about the process of soul reckoning. The perfectly righteous person might have a "perfect record," but if she hasn't done *teshuvah*, she may not have the depth or soulfulness of the penitent. The perfectly righteous person could be akin to a very finely tuned machine, programmed to perform morally under all circumstances. But only the penitent has the merit that comes with self-scrutiny and self-love.

A related possibility is that the penitent has a higher status than the wholly righteous individual because "the reward is according to the trouble" (*Pirkei Avot* 5:25). By analogy, the naturally gifted athlete who can set a world record with relative ease does not earn as much admiration from us as the less-gifted competitor who trains far harder and longer just to come in second. The work involved in overcoming obstacles has its own intrinsic virtue. To the wholly righteous person, doing what is right may be effortless. Only the penitent knows what it takes to get up each morning and do battle with the evil impulse, as well as the satisfaction of constructing a new moral life out of the ruins of a failed one.

One final interpretation builds upon the transformative quality of *teshuvah* for an explanation of Abbahu's striking teaching. Adin Steinsaltz offers this explanation:

> The highest level of repentance, however, lies beyond the correction of sinful deeds and the creation of independent, new patterns that counterweigh past sins and injuries.... This level of *tikun* [repair, transformation] is reached when a person draws from his failings not only the ability to do good, but the power to fall again and again and, notwithstanding, to transform more extensive and important segments of life. It is using the knowledge of the sin of the past and transforming it into such an extraordinary thirst for good that it becomes a Divine force. The more a man was sunken in evil, the more eager he becomes for good.... This is the significance of the statement in the Talmud that in the place where a completely

repentant person stands, even the most saintly cannot enter; because the penitent has at his disposal not only the forces of good in his soul and in the world, but also those of evil, which he transforms into essences of holiness.[16]

According to this view, the penitent is higher than the wholly righteous person because she has harnessed the forces of evil within her and redeemed them, turning them into forces for goodness. The righteous person is powered, as it were, only by the forces of good, while the penitent has unleashed the energy of the evil impulse as well and channeled it into righteousness. We do not earn a demerit when we transgress as long as we repent and thereby use our failure as the occasion to uncover more and more elements within us that have inclined us to evil in the past and now can be redirected toward a life of good deeds.

In a world where only results matter, we could never put the penitent above the person with a perfect record. But that is not the world in which we live. The practice of repentance itself is meant to teach us this. For repentance invites us to live in a world where process takes precedence over product, effort over perfection. Above all, it invites us to see our failures as opportunities to transform ourselves by transforming the roots of evil within us into sources of goodness.

48

Repentance and Redemption

Rabbi Yohanan said, "Great is repentance, for it
brings redemption, as it is said: 'A redeemer will
come to Zion, and unto them that turn from transgression in Jacob' (Isaiah 59:20)...." We have been
taught that Rabbi Meir used to say, "Great is repentance, for on account of one individual who vows
repentance, pardon is given to him as well as to
the entire world, to all of it, as it is said, 'I will heal
their backsliding, I will love them freely, when my
anger is turned away from him' (Hosea 14:5).
Hosea does not say, 'From them,' but, 'From him.'"

Babylonian Talmud, *Yoma* 86b

The connection between repentance and redemption is easy to
understand. Both involve a process of turning to God and
reestablishing a relationship of trust and loyalty. The difference
would seem to lie only in the frame of reference: repentance is an
individual matter, while redemption concerns the Jewish people
and ultimately the world as a whole. But these Talmudic teachings say more than just that these two processes mirror one
another, operating, as it were, on parallel planes. Rather, they
claim that individual repentance actually brings national redemption. How can this be so?

If we think again about the path of repentance, we realize that
the goal of *teshuvah* is a three-tiered process of healing. Penitents
reclaim a lost sense of integrity and wholeness within themselves,
repair broken relationships with those they have injured, and return

to God, the Source of all life and goodness. Psychologically, ethically, and spiritually, repentance is all about healing, a restoration of the situation that existed within us, among us, and between us and God before our transgressions undermined those relationships.

In another sense, though, *teshuvah*, as we have seen, involves the creation of something altogether new and unprecedented. Penitents were sometimes known to take new names to indicate that they were utterly new people. Hasidic sources in particular emphasize that *teshuvah* is less about the repair of something broken than it is about the possibility of completely transcending the past. In this way the penitent can create a new reality that makes it as though the transgressions of the past never happened at all.

Both of these views have their place in theories of redemption. Gershom Scholem, the twentieth century's greatest scholar of Jewish mysticism, explained that Jewish messianism encompasses both "restorative" and "utopian" dimensions. By this he meant that the ultimate culmination of history, which biblical and Rabbinic sources have always connected with the coming of a messianic figure, was sometimes imagined as a return to an idyllic state (the closeness that God and Israel experienced at Sinai, for example) and sometimes as a new state of being utterly unlike anything that has ever existed before (when we will choose to obey God's laws willingly and consistently).[17] Either way, redemption is a transformative process. Our current state of existence, marked by struggle, transgression, and discord, is to give way to a condition of peace, obedience, and harmony.

In a sense, then, repentance and redemption are less parallel processes than two parts of a single process. The restorative and/or utopian forces at work in the world transcend both individuals and nations. In the words of Rabbi Soloveitchik:

> For what is redemption from exile? Redemption means returning to one's true origins. The sinner has removed himself from his roots, his origin; repentance serves to restore him to the source of his being. As in spiritual redemption, so it is in bodily redemption—the ingathering of the exiles and repentance, two things which are really one.[18]

Return and renewal are the essence of God's desire for the world as a whole and also for all individuals within it. The great drama of human history and the drama that unfolds in the privacy of an individual's soul are the very same drama viewed macroscopically and microscopically, as it were.

But we might also see the relationship between repentance and redemption as sequential. As each of us does our individual work of transformation, we bring the world as a whole closer to redemption. Indeed, the latter depends entirely on the former. The world as a whole cannot be perfected until we do the individual work of repentance that uproots the influence of the evil impulse in our lives. This is what the Rabbis meant when they taught:

> The world is judged by the majority [of its deeds], and an individual is likewise judged by the majority [of his deeds].... If a person performs one good deed, happy is he, for he has tilted the scale both for himself and for the entire world, all of it, toward the side of merit. If he commits even one transgression, woe to him, for he has tilted the scale both for himself and for the entire world, all of it, toward the scale of guilt.
>
> **(Babylonian Talmud, *Kiddushin* 40b)**

There is an arithmetic logic at work here that is inescapable. Humanity as a whole can only move toward redemption when individuals do their part. The transformation of individual penitents through repentance, then, is primary and, as one of its consequences, contributes to the transformation of redemption.

But there is still another sense in which the individual's repentance affects the world at large. The Rabbis frequently invoke the concept of "the merit of the forefathers" (*zechut avot*). Israel is redeemed by God, not by virtue of their own deeds, but by virtue of the merits of Abraham, Isaac, and Jacob. In the words of one classical Rabbinic source, "The Holy One said, 'Israel has no good deeds that would justify their redemption, other than the merit of their elders'" (Exodus Rabbah 15:4). The reasoning here is spiritual rather than arithmetic or causal. Some people stand in a special relationship to God such that their good deeds transcend their own lives and radiate down through the generations, benefitting infinite generations after them.[19]

This notion of vicarious merit is behind the startling statement of Rabbi Meir in the opening epigraph. The power of penitence extends outward beyond the individual who engages in it to the benefit of all people. Just as the individual sinner can point to the merits of Abraham, Isaac, and Jacob, saying to God, in effect, "Do not judge me on my own merits alone, but consider me as part of a people that includes these righteous ancestors, and allow their merit to help offset my deficits," so too can he point to the merits of all penitents. When we fear that God might just give up on us, either individually or collectively, we can appeal to the example of the penitent, whose righteousness proves that there is still hope for us. Each penitent demonstrates to God that profound personal transformation is truly possible, and this, in turn, is proof positive that humanity as a whole is worth redeeming. Just as God was once prepared to spare Sodom and Gomorrah for the sake of ten righteous individuals (Genesis 18:32), so too will God look favorably upon the world as a whole on account of the penitents among us. In precisely this way, the repentance of a single individual makes redemption more likely for us all.

49

The Mystery of *Teshuvah*

> Repentance cannot be comprehended rationally;
> it does not really make sense. Even the angels do
> not understand what repentance is.
>
> **Rabbi Joseph B. Soloveitchik**[20]

There is a paradox at the heart of *teshuvah*. The past, which should be immutable, can be changed. Through repentance the wrongs we have committed can be undone and even, if we believe the mystics, turned into sources of goodness. It is as if someone announced to us one day that God had given us the power, all on our own, to defy the laws of causality, to overturn the law of gravity in the moral sphere. It should not be possible, and yet it is. Jewish tradition affirms that it is so, and my own experience and that of many others I have known confirm those teachings. Repentance is real. But how can our mind comprehend what our heart has discovered?

In truth, this paradox is but one of many. As we have seen, Judaism teaches that *teshuvah* forces us to take responsibility for the past, even as it promises us freedom from that past. It seems, in fact, that our ability to overcome the mistakes of the past increases in direct proportion to our determination to own them. Paradoxically, we can escape the burdens of our past only by running toward them, rather than away from them.

Still more, the person who has been burdened with guilt and habituated to moral failing can be reborn, emerging as a person of integrity, self-awareness, and moral insight. Anyone who has witnessed such a radical transformation could be excused for believing the words of Ezekiel:

> I will give you a new heart and put a new spirit within you: I will remove the heart of stone from your body and give you a heart of flesh; and I will put My spirit into you. Thus I will cause you to follow My laws and faithfully to observe My rules.
>
> **(Ezekiel 36:26–27)**

It is hard to explain the mechanism by which such transformations take place, other than to credit some supernatural force at work in human life. Penitents exhibit a kind of radical freedom that seems to be evidence of grace, that is, a gift that comes to us from another realm. Perhaps it is evidence that God's own freedom has been implanted within the human soul, and after a long dormant period, it awakens and gives the penitent a power to change that surprises everyone, no one more than the penitent herself.

If we lived in another age, a time less obsessed with technology and science, we would readily turn to the language of miracles to explain such profound transformations. But miracles are out of fashion these days. In fact, most contemporary Jews, among others, have long since quit believing that God intervenes in history or the natural world in the sorts of dramatic ways recorded in the Bible. It is easier to believe that the world operates according to laws that are susceptible to rational explanation, that what in earlier times were called miracles were just events that people could not yet explain or that never actually happened at all.

But perhaps even in our largely secular age we can still find room to believe in a spiritual power that is sometimes at work in our souls, with profound results. This does not require that we suspend our commitment to rational explanation entirely, only that we concede what seems self-evident—sometimes, without explanation, people who are terminally ill long outlive their physician's expectation, and sometimes people who have long been mired in transgression, unaware of themselves and insensitive to others, engage in a process of *teshuvah* and emerge morally transformed.

Whether they change their names or not, it is evident to all that they are different people.

Here, finally, is where the metaphor of walking the path of repentance breaks down. When we walk along a path, we can look back and retrace our steps. But movement along the path of repentance is rarely so evident or sequential. The soul is not bound by the temporal or spatial limitations that require us to be here before we can be there. A simple gesture, a leap of faith, a word of affirmation can transport the soul—sometimes dramatically, sometimes imperceptibly—to a new place where transformations formerly unimaginable become possible or even irresistible. Such is the nature of *teshuvah*, that it unfolds in places inaccessible to empirical observation and in ways impervious to rational analysis.

There is an alchemy in *teshuvah*. It turns the dross of human souls into gold, though not to be sure through any incantations or magical formulas. The turning from evil to good is in some ways the simplest of acts. But then, so too is breathing. Any physician can readily explain the mechanism by which we inhale and exhale, exchanging oxygen and carbon dioxide. But the fact that we are living, breathing creatures at all—that human life in all its splendor and complexity exists in the first place—this is not finally explicable in material terms alone. As Abraham Joshua Heschel wrote, the fact that there is anything at all rather than nothing is a source of radical amazement.[21] So, too, is the reality of *teshuvah*.

In the presence of *teshuvah* we do well to set aside the search for explanations, for none would finally satisfy us. Rather, let us acknowledge the miracle that *teshuvah* is possible, witness its transformative power in our lives, and express our awe and gratitude for the opportunities it affords us.

Conclusion
Teshuvah in Our Time

The problem of sin persists. Whether we look at the private lives of individuals, where parents still abandon and abuse their children; the practices of corporations, where corruption is rampant; or the conduct of nations, where injustice and cover-ups are prevalent, the world is rife with sinful behavior. Clergy, too, have been caught up in scandal to a remarkable degree, as evidenced by the Roman Catholic priests found guilty of sexual abuse and by the Orthodox rabbis indicted for violating labor laws, abusing illegal immigrants, and participating in political corruption. Everywhere we turn, it seems, the moral fabric of our society is coming undone. And this is all just the commonplace sinfulness we encounter every day, before we begin to contemplate the enormity of genocide in Rwanda and Darfur or the fact that we tolerate a world in which over a billion people lack clean drinking water.

I do not mean to suggest that people are fundamentally more depraved today than they were in ages past. In fact, any careful reading of history would likely reveal that people are prone to transgression in roughly equal degrees, in fairly comparable ways, irrespective of time period, culture, religious affiliation, or any other factor. This confirms what our religious and moral teachers have been telling us since they first began reflecting on the human condition: sinfulness has been and continues to be an irreducible part of our humanity. Until the messianic redemption arrives, we are all sinners, to one degree or another.

The true test of the spiritual maturity of a civilization, then, is not really the level of its moral behavior, but the way it responds to moral misbehavior. The critical questions are these:

How deeply do we reflect upon the problem of human transgression? How sophisticated and honest is our public discourse on our moral failings? How rigorously do we hold people accountable for their misdeeds, and how actively do we encourage people to make amends for their errors?

When we ask ourselves these questions, the answers, I'm afraid, are not encouraging. There is widespread evidence that we have lost touch with much of what our western religious traditions have taught us about transgression and moral transformation. The practice of repentance is something of a lost art, and what is worse, most people appear to be unaware that it is lost and so are oblivious to the resulting moral impoverishment of our society. We rightly bemoan the loss of native arts, close-knit families, and the handwritten personal letter. But who among us protests that we have lost the fine art of public apology or the courage required to engage in serious soul reckoning? For all our technological and intellectual sophistication, we have become handicapped morally by our failure to nurture the habits of heart and soul that are required for addressing the moral mistakes that we inevitably make.

The evidence of this failure is all around us. I'd like to suggest that our society's response to moral transgressions tends to fall into one of three categories: avoidance, trivialization, and moralizing. Each of these responses, I think, testifies eloquently to the poverty of our collective understanding of the practice and meaning of repentance.

Those who avoid repentance are perhaps the easiest to identify and criticize. I have already mentioned the prevalence of politicians and businesspeople accused of wrongdoing who adamantly protest their innocence and assure us, sometimes through their attorneys, that they are eager for all the facts to come out so that they can be exonerated. And, almost invariably, when they have their day in court, the facts are pretty much as they seemed—they stand guilty as accused, only now we know that their professed innocence was nothing but an elaborate show designed to preserve a public facade of rectitude a little longer. They continue to act in bad faith because they are incapable of admitting their wrongs in public and atoning for them; perhaps some have even convinced themselves through some mechanism of self-deception that they really are innocent. What we know is that they are not honest or humble, two of the virtues required for genuine contrition, self-disclosure, apology, and reconciliation. Some of them appear childish, others fiendish. But all of them are clueless about what repentance is.[1]

Only slightly less clueless are the trivializers, those who make an effort at repentance, but one that is halfhearted, defensive, or otherwise ineffective. In the end, they only succeed in cheapening the whole process of repentance. They offer an apology, but in a way that is conditional ("I am sorry if I have offended you") or that subtly shifts the blame to the other party ("I am sorry that you felt hurt by my actions") or that simply is at odds with the facts (as when they claim that their behavior was accidental when, in fact, it is part of a well-established pattern). In these and a thousand other ways large and small, people can express remorse without really feeling it or claim to be repairing a broken relationship without doing the hard work that is required. But most of us know the difference between empty gestures of repentance and the real thing, and moral counterfeits are no more welcome than monetary ones. Such people give repentance a bad name, for they lead others to believe that all (or, at least, most) gestures of repentance are just that—gestures without substance. And once people come to think of repentance as largely worthless, they will rightly quit caring whether anyone even pretends to engage in it.

Of course, it is possible to trivialize repentance in even more blatant and grotesque ways. We need only think of those ever-popular TV shows on which people are invited to confess their sins in public for the entertainment of the audience.[2] To the extent that there is even a pretense of engaging in repentance here, these displays can only be regarded as a mockery of real repentance. For genuine repentance is a serious business that requires profound soul reckoning; it is born of brokenheartedness and remorse, and it happens, if at all, only in moments of profound intimacy between the offender and those the offender has hurt. Real repentance is not a made-for-TV drama designed to shock an audience or play to their voyeuristic instincts.

Finally, there are the moralists who have no time for repentance altogether, who say that those who have sinned must be held accountable, without hesitation and without mercy. Such people can be found among those who take a hard line on criminals, who insist that they be stripped of their rights, who believe that we should "lock them up and throw away the key." For such people, of course, "sinners" are always others, in a separate category, safely distinguishable from the rest of us. The moralists affirm that it is good and right that convicted felons be forever deprived of their rights to vote, hold public office, be admitted to the bar, practice medicine, or otherwise participate fully in the life of society, notwithstanding whatever they may have done to repent for their crimes.[3] Life is simpler and our moral categories are neater if we don't allow for the possibility of repentance at all. For the practice of repentance presupposes that all of us (sometimes) transgress and all of us (always) have the freedom to change.

To be sure, the situation is not entirely so bleak. There are hopeful signs in some quarters that the meaning and power of repentance are appreciated. The famous Truth and Reconciliation Commission in South Africa, for all its shortcomings, demonstrated the possibility that there is the potential for enormous social healing when perpetrators are encouraged to confess their deeds publicly. The very fact that similar efforts have been undertaken (in Rwanda, Argentina, Brazil, and Germany, among other places) attests that the art of repentance is alive and well, especially in countries that have been torn apart by ethnic violence and genocide. So, too, do the apologies issued in 1988 by the United States to Japanese Americans for the internment camps established during World War II,[4] the similar apology issued in 1997 to African Americans abused in the Tuskeegee experiments on the effects of untreated syphilis,[5] and Pope John Paul II's apology in 2000 for the sins of those who acted in the name of the Roman Catholic Church.[6] The entire movement associated with "restorative justice" has also developed in recent years as an alternative to more traditional retributive models of criminal justice. Its advocates, who explicitly draw on models of repentance, recognize that remorse and restitution, together with a direct encounter between the perpetrators and victims of a crime, can enable the reintegration of the offender into society.[7]

For all these reasons, it would surely be an exaggeration to declare that the way of repentance is dead. But just as surely, it is far from thriving. The irony—some might say, the tragedy—of all this is that the wisdom we most deeply need, as individuals and as a society, is readily available to us, if we only take the time to study and absorb it. Our religious traditions have long understood the nature of transgression and the need to overcome it, and they have prepared a well-worn path to help us find the wholeness and reconciliation we seek.

As we have seen, Jewish sources point us toward a middle path, away from the simplistic alternatives of easy grace, according to which transgression is not a serious problem, and of rigid moralism, according to which moral failings are irredeemable. In the former case, *teshuvah* is not necessary; in the latter case, it is not possible. But we can afford to be neither so cavalier with respect to our transgressions nor so severe in our condemnation of the sinner along with the sin. What we need instead is the demand that we take our failings with the utmost seriousness, but that we take equal account of our ability to overcome them. What we need is the path of repentance.

The alternatives have led us into a quandary that has paralyzed our public lives. On the one hand, we permit criminals to confess their crimes, turn government witness, and avoid most penalties for their deeds. We allow others to plea-bargain, so that they confess to less serious crimes than the ones they committed and therefore never actually pay the price for their transgressions. And most of all we allow the flimsiest of defenses to exonerate those who commit serious crimes—the famous "Twinkie defense" in the trial of Dan White for the murders of George Moscone, mayor of San Francisco, and Harvey Milk, is perhaps the prime example. In all these ways, we fail to hold people accountable for their transgressions.

Yet, we also find ourselves trapped in precisely the opposite reaction. We refuse to tolerate even the smallest failings in our public figures. Someone who admits to smoking marijuana in his youth is declared unfit to hold public office, leading Bill Clinton to insist famously, and surely dishonestly, that he "didn't inhale." We insist that the politician who made a mistake in paying his income taxes must resign, even after the monies owed have been repaid, and the one who had an extramarital affair must likewise resign, even after he has publicly confessed and his wife has forgiven him. Even when the offense is relatively minor, and the effort to apologize for it seems sincere, there are some who would insist that no repentance is possible or, at least, none is sufficient to restore an offender to her former status.

We seem to bounce back and forth between a pervasive failure to hold people accountable and an equally powerful obsession with doing so. It is as though we have lost our moral equilibrium. We can no longer find a proper balance between insisting on justice and insisting that, once the demands of justice have been met, compassion be extended to the offender. But Judaism offers us a third way, which marries accountability for the past with freedom from the past. It takes sin seriously, but no more seriously than the perennial opportunity to overcome it. For these two dimensions of human life are finally not opposed, but complementary. In *teshuvah*, accountability and freedom are revealed to be equally necessary and interdependent. We need to find inner wholeness, make peace with our neighbors, and sustain a connection with God.

In the final analysis, human nature being what it is, we will continue to need the interlocking concepts of guilt and repentance. The former indicates that we have internalized the moral law and recognize when we have transgressed it; the latter indicates our determination to restore, both in ourselves and in relationship to others, what we have broken. To mitigate the sense of guilt is to risk social and moral chaos, for it allows us to indulge the fantasy that everything is permitted. But to deny the possibility of repentance is to deny the need for and reality of human freedom. It is to suppose that, individually and collectively, we are enslaved to the past. In classical Christian terms, we need both law and grace, moral limits (which, when transgressed, yield guilt and remorse) and moral freedom, which, through repentance, enables us to correct our transgressions and repair ourselves and our world. *Teshuvah* is the means by which we marry law and grace, accountability and freedom, responsibility for the past and openness to the future.

Our lives are marked not by our achievements, or certainly not by them alone, but rather by how we deal with our failures, especially our moral failings. Revealing to the world only our virtues, our achievements, the things that make us "proud," contributes to our own moral impoverishment. For when we do not bring all of ourselves, our faults in particular, into the open, we not only conceal ourselves from those we love most, but we also become partially invisible even to ourselves. Worse yet, we come to believe that what is concealed in this way does not really matter, that the facade of goodness and rectitude that we present is the whole of who we are. Then, in those quiet moments of self-reflection when the lights on the stage of our lives have gone dark and we find ourselves alone with our thoughts, we confront the harsh truth—that we live bifurcated lives, that our lives lack wholeness and integrity. We not only deceive and falsify from time to time, but in a fundamental way we also live a lie.

It is into this dark and painful reality that *teshuvah* comes with its startling message of hope—that there is a way out of this truncated and stultifying life; indeed, that there is but one way out. But that road to wholeness and integrity—with ourselves, our neighbors, and God—lies in the commitment to truthfulness, responsibility, and humility. And, better yet, that following this path brings not only reconciliation but also a return to the person we most deeply, truly are and were created to be. *Teshuvah* in this sense is a true homecoming, which is simultaneously a turning away from transgression and brokenness and a turning toward the ones we have harmed, turning inward to ourselves but also toward God, who loves us even in our waywardness and calls us to truthfulness and wholeness.

For anyone who has encountered these teachings on *teshuvah*, there can be no question of how to begin the process of repentance. The path is carefully laid out, including the obstacles we are likely to encounter along the way and the strategies others have used to overcome them. Nor can there really be much question about the meaning and value of *teshuvah*, for these too have been expounded from Talmudic times to our own day. From those who have claimed that *teshuvah* was woven into the fabric of the universe even before creation to those who have praised *teshuvah* as giving us access to divine energies, repentance retains its honored place as the key to moral rehabilitation and reconciliation, both divine and human.

The only question left unanswered is the question that can only be answered in the depths of each person's heart: how shall I finally find the will to undertake the arduous work of *teshuvah* and then, because I will inevitably fail, to begin it yet again? The path of repentance will be, by turns, difficult and easy, straightforward and circuitous. But, like all spiritual paths, the most difficult part may be the decision to embark upon the journey in the first place. There is much holding us back—fear, to be sure, but also shame, pride, and hopelessness. In this respect, we may take some comfort from one final text. It is the biblical text that is read in synagogues each year on the Shabbat before Rosh Hashanah. In one of Moses's final addresses to the Israelites, he admonishes them one last time that God will bless them if they observe the law and curse them if they depart from it. He reminds them of the great gift of the Promised Land that they are about to enter and possess. He encourages them to love God and to "return to the LORD your God with all your heart and soul" (Deuteronomy 30:10), a phrase that echoes the theme of returning and repentance that marks this season of the year.

And then, anticipating the reticence of the Israelites to believe that all this is possible and to commit themselves to living by the terms of the covenant, Moses says:

> Surely this Instruction which I enjoin upon you this day is not too baffling for you, nor is it beyond reach. It is not in the heavens, that you should say, "Who among us can go up to the heavens and get it for us and impart it to us, that we may observe it?" Neither is it beyond the sea, that you should say, "Who among us can cross to the other side of the sea and get it for us and impart it to us, that we may observe it?" No, the thing is very close to you, in your mouth and in your heart, to observe it.

(Deuteronomy 30:11–14)

May all who read these words and study these texts find the courage and willingness to take them to heart and embrace the way of *teshuvah*, with contrition for the past and with hope for the future.

Notes

Introduction: Exploring *Teshuvah*

1. Jacob Neusner, "Repentance in Judaism," in *The Encyclopedia of Judaism*, ed. Jacob Neusner, Alan J. Avery-Peck, and William Scott Green (Leiden: E. J. Brill, 2000), 3:1255.
2. Ehud Luz, "Repentance," in *Contemporary Jewish Religious Thought*, ed. Arthur A. Cohen and Paul Mendes-Flohr (New York: Scribner, 1987), 785.
3. I discuss Jewish views of forgiveness in my article "The Quality of Mercy: On the Duty to Forgive in the Judaic Tradition," *Journal of Religious Ethics* 15, no. 2 (1987):155–72.
4. See, for example, Solomon Schechter, *Aspects of Rabbinic Theology* (New York: Schocken, 1961; originally published 1909); Louis Jacobs, *Jewish Theology* (West Orange, NJ: Behrman House, 1973); Samuel Belkin, *In His Image* (London: Abelard-Schuman, 1960). By contrast, see Ehud Luz, "Repentance," in *Contemporary Jewish Religious Thought*, ed. Arthur A. Cohen and Paul Mendes-Flohr (New York: Charles Scribner's Sons, 1987), 785–93 for a nuanced analysis of different dimensions of the concept of *teshuvah*.

Part I: The Nature of Sin

1. For further discussions of this metaphor, see Pinchas H. Peli, *Soloveitchik on Repentance* (New York: Paulist Press, 1984), 146–52, 192ff.; see also Paul Ricoeur, *The Symbolism of Evil* (Boston: Beacon Press, 1967), 86–87.
2. Broad generalizations in the history of religions are notoriously difficult to support, but there is some evidence to suggest that certain classical Christian writers tend to take the existential condition of human sinfulness more seriously than do Jewish thinkers, insofar as the governing metaphor is death, rather than illness. Accordingly, Jewish thinkers appear to take repentance as a remedy for sin more seriously than do their Christian counterparts. Consider Maimonides' statement that "there is no sin so great that it can withstand the power of *teshuvah*" (*Mishneh Torah*, Laws of *Teshuvah* 3:14) as against

Kierkegaard's statement that "repentance cannot cancel sin, it can only sorrow over it. Sin advances in its consequence; repentance follows it step by step, but always a moment too late" (Søren Kierkegaard, *The Concept of Anxiety*, trans. Reidar Thomte [Princeton, NJ: Princeton University Press, 1980], 115).

3. Peli, *Soloveitchik on Repentance*, 82.
4. Martin Buber, *Hasidism and Modern Man* (Atlantic Highlands, NJ: Humanities Press International, 1988), 167.
5. Ricoeur, *Symbolism of Evil*, 25.
6. Paul Tillich, the great twentieth-century Protestant theologian, defined idolatry this way: "In true faith the ultimate concern is a concern about the truly ultimate; while in idolatrous faith preliminary, finite realities are elevated to the rank of ultimacy" (*Dynamics of Faith* [New York: Harper and Row, 1958], 12).
7. Augustine, Homily 7 on First Epistle of John (1 John 4:4–12).
8. The "Big Book" of Alcoholics Anonymous puts it this way: "Those who do not recover are people who cannot or will not completely give themselves to this simple program ... they are naturally incapable of grasping and developing a manner of living which demands rigorous honesty" (Alcoholics Anonymous World Services, *The Big Book Online*, 2009, 58).

Part II: Release from Sin

1. Reinhold Niebuhr, "The Assurance of Grace," in *The Essential Reinhold Niebuhr*, ed. Robert McAfee Brown (New Haven: Yale University Press, 1986), 68.
2. Walther Eichrodt, *Man in the Old Testament* (London: SCM Press, 1951), 15.
3. Ricoeur, *Symbolism of Evil*, 94.
4. Edmund Leach, "The Logic of Sacrifice," in *Anthropological Approaches to the Old Testament*, ed. Bernhard Lang (Philadelphia: Fortress, 1985), 145.
5. Peli, *Soloveitchik on Repentance*, 246.
6. John C. Lyden, "Atonement in Judaism and Christianity: Toward a Rapprochement," *Journal of Ecumenical Studies* 29, no. 1 (1992): 48.
7. Peli, *Soloveitchik on Repentance*, 242.
8. The physical meaning of "cover" is retained in the related word, *kaporet*, which signified the covering over the ark in the tabernacle (Exodus 25:17ff.). This gold covering may bear this name, as well, because it plays a central role in the rituals of atonement performed on Yom Kippur.
9. The precise meaning of Azazel and the significance of the whole rite has been the subject of controversy for centuries. Some suggest that Azazel is the name of a demon that lives in the wilderness to whom

the sins of the people are sent through a kind of exorcism. Others suggest that Azazel is merely the name of a place, perhaps once associated with a demon, but now merely a place outside the realm of the community to which the people's sins are banished. See Jacob Milgrom, *Leviticus*, Anchor Bible Series (New York: Doubleday, 1991), esp. 1071ff.

10. In this sense, suffering is a kind of sacrifice, and in fact, the Rabbis sometimes drew that analogy explicitly. See Babylonian Talmud, *Chullin* 7b: any loss of blood through accident atones as blood of sacrifice.

11. See Ecclesiastes Rabbah 7:27 for a discussion of various types of suffering that would constitute paying your debt to heaven for your sins. Of course, the acceptance of this logic does not preclude praying to be spared from this painful way of atoning for sins. One such prayer includes the following: "May You in Your infinite mercy clear me of my sins, but not by means of suffering and terrible illness...." The author of this prayer recognized that suffering could lead to atonement but hoped that some less painful method might achieve the same end.

12. This view carries with it the potential danger that we could imagine death as offering automatic expiation for all our sins, which would undermine the imperative to act ethically throughout our life. In this sense, the teaching of *Mishnah, Yoma* 8:9 would apply (see chap. 37—we cannot sin with impunity and then rely on the rituals of atonement to cancel our transgressions). Dying, whether literally or figuratively, brings freedom from the power of sin. Christianity embraces a figurative concept of death in the language of "dying to sin," which is so prevalent in the writings of Paul (see Romans 6:6–7, 6:10–11). The Christian is invited to "die" as Jesus died and thereby achieve the freedom from sin that he experienced, precisely so that she can be "reborn" as Jesus was resurrected, and so attain eternal salvation.

Part III: The Way of *Teshuvah*

1. This translation is the one generally found in liturgical contexts where readers are most likely to encounter this quotation.

2. The JPS translation has "shun evil," but this translation better captures the sense of moving away from evil.

3. See Aaron Lazare, *On Apology* (New York: Oxford University Press, 2004), for an insightful discussion of successful and failed apologies.

4. Abraham Isaac Kook, *Lights of Penitence*, trans. Ben Zion Bokser (New York: Paulist Press, 1978), 119–20.

5. 'Abd al-Karim al-Qushayri, *Principles of Sufism*, trans. Barbara R. Von Schlegell (Berkeley, CA: Mizan Press 1992), 1.

6. Max Scheler articulated this idea in a more philosophical idiom: "For it is the peculiar nature of repentance that in the very act which is so painfully destructive we gain our first complete insight into the badness of our self and conduct, and that in the same act which seems rationally comprehensible only from the 'freer' vantage point of the new plane of existence, this very vantage point is attained. So the act of repentance precedes in a certain sense both its point of departure and its point of arrival, its *terminus a quo* and its *terminus ad quem*" (*On the Eternal in Man* [New York: Harper and Brothers, 1960], 47).

7. Harold O. J. Brown, "Godly Sorrow, Sorrow of the World: Some Christian Thoughts on Repentance," in *Repentance: A Comparative Perspective*, ed. Amitai Etzioni and David E. Carney (Lanham, NY: Rowman and Littlefield, 1997), 39.

8. Peli, *Soloveitchik on Repentance*, 95.

9. Richard Cross, "Atonement without Satisfaction," *Religious Studies* 37, no. 4 (December 2001): 403.

10. Abu Nasr as-Sarraj, *Kitab al-Luma' (The Book of Flashes)*, in *Early Islamic Mysticism*, trans. Michael A. Sells (New York: Paulist Press, 1996), 199.

11. These two studies appeared as "Beneath the Robe: The Role of Personal Values in Judicial Ethics," *Journal of Law and Religion* 12, no. 2 (1995–96):507–31; and "Ethics, Faith and Healing: Jewish Physicians Reflect on Medical Practice," in *Caring Well: Religion, Narrative and Health Care Ethics*, ed. David H. Smith (Louisville, KY: Westminster John Knox Press, 2000), 117–43.

12. Peli, *Soloveitchik on Repentance*, 253.

Part IV: *Teshuvah* in Three Dimensions

1. Although repentance in the broadest sense actually encompasses all three dimensions discussed here—psychological, ethical, and spiritual—I suspect that this inner work was understood by the Rabbis as the essence of "turning." In that sense, when they wrote of "repentance, prayer, and righteousness," I think that the first element in this triad may well have referred primarily to this psychological component in the process.

2. Erich Fromm, *Man for Himself: An Inquiry into the Psychology of Ethics* (New York: Holt, Rinehart and Winston, 1947), 233.

3. Abraham H. Maslow, *Toward a Psychology of Being*, 2nd ed. (New York: D. Van Nostrand, 1968), 160–61.

4. Rollo May, *Man's Search for Himself* (New York: W. W. Norton, 1953), 144.

5. Maslow, *Toward a Psychology of Being*, 165–66.

6. Carl R. Rogers, *On Becoming a Person* (Boston: Houghton Mifflin, 1961), 175–76.

7. Roman Catholicism teaches, "Sin is before all else an offense against God, a rupture of communion with Him. At the same time it damages communion with the Church. For this reason conversion entails both God's forgiveness and reconciliation with the Church, which are expressed and accomplished liturgically by the sacrament of Penance and Reconciliation" (*Catechism of the Catholic Church* [Mahwah, NJ: Paulist Press, 1994], 1440, p. 361). Of course, Catholic teaching also requires that "one must do what is possible in order to repair the harm [to our neighbors]" (1459, p. 366). But God's forgiveness does not appear to be contingent upon such acts of restitution.

8. Kook, *Lights of Penitence*, 117.

9. Henry David Thoreau, *Walden*, in *The Portable Thoreau*, ed. Carl Bode (New York: Viking Press, 1947), 343.

10. Peli, *Soloveitchik on Repentance*, 185.

Part V: Experiencing *Teshuvah*

1. Phillipa Foot, *Virtues and Vices* (Berkeley and Los Angeles: University of California Press, 1978), 4.

2. Peli, *Soloveitchik on Repentance*, 116.

3. Rabbi Bachya ben Joseph ibn Pakuda, *Duties of the Heart*, trans. Moses Hyamson (New York: Feldheim, 1970), 2:125.

4. Ibid., 2:89.

5. For a general discussion of Christian attitudes toward sin, see Alistair McFadyen, "Sin," in *Oxford Companion to Christian Thought*, ed. Adrian Hastings (New York: Oxford University Press, 2000), 665–8.

6. Abraham Joshua Heschel, *God in Search of Man* (New York: Farrar, Straus and Giroux, 1955), 336–47.

7. Kook, *Lights of Penitence*, 113.

8. Nachman of Breslov, *Likutei Moharan*, Tanina, 112.

9. Peli, *Soloveitchik on Repentance*, 254–55.

10. Kook, *Lights of Penitence*, 70–71.

11. Adin Steinsaltz, *The Strife of the Spirit* (Northvale, NJ: Jason Aronson, 1988), 101.

Part VI: *Teshuvah:* Its Problems and Limits

1. Mahmoud Ayoub, "Repentance in the Islamic Tradition," in *Repentance: A Comparative Perspective*, ed. Amitai Etzioni and David E. Carney (Lanham, NY: Rowman and Littlefield, 1998), 102.

2. There are many ways of reading Jonah's motivation for fleeing when asked to prophecy to the Ninevites. Perhaps he wants to protect the Israelites from looking bad because they do not so readily repent as the Ninevites do. Alternatively, he may be attempting to

save God from looking fickle (or soft) for so readily forgiving the Ninevites. Still again, he may be motivated by self-interest, in that he will look bad if he predicts Nineveh's downfall only to be proven wrong when God relents and saves them. Whichever way we read Jonah's intentions, the implicit assumption seems to be that it would be better if Nineveh got what it deserved than if they repented and God forgave them.

3. A similar point about God's overriding compassion emerges from this striking midrash: "They asked Wisdom, 'What is the punishment of the sinner?' Wisdom answered, 'Evil pursues sinners' (Proverbs 13:21). They asked Prophecy, 'What is the punishment of the sinner?' Prophecy answered, 'The soul that sins, it shall die' (Ezekiel 18:4). They asked the Torah, 'What is the punishment of the sinner?' Torah answered, 'Let him bring a guilt-offering and it shall be forgiven unto him....' (Leviticus 1:4). They asked the Holy One, blessed be God, 'What is the punishment of the sinner?' The Holy One, blessed be God, answered, 'Let him do repentance and it shall be forgiven unto him'" (Jerusalem Talmud, *Makkot* 31d).

4. More accurately, this is one of the Rabbis' views, for they often express the opposite view, that the gates of repentance are always open. Indeed, the latter may be the more widely accepted view.

5. Some argue that this theological view is supported by the language of the Exodus narrative. They note that early in the narrative the language generally is that "Pharaoh's heart was hardened" (Exodus 7:13–14, 7:22, 8:11, 8:15, 8:28, 9:7, 9:34–35, 13:15), while later in the narrative the language shifts to "God hardened Pharaoh's heart" (Exodus 4:21, 7:3, 9:12, 10:1, 10:20, 10:27, 11:10, 14:4, 14:8, 14:17). But the pattern is not completely consistent, because the language of God's hardening the heart appears at the very outset of the story, before Pharaoh has had any opportunity to repent (Exodus 4:21, 7:3). So this may be a distinction without a difference. Moreover, the biblical author's overarching point seems to be that God is the sole author of Israel's history. Lest we be inclined to attribute the Israelites' liberation from slavery to Pharaoh's largesse, the text goes to great lengths to remind us that God controlled the whole process, much as God controlled the whole natural order, through plagues and miracles. According to the author of the Exodus narrative, it seems, God wasn't interested in Pharaoh's repenting at the outset of the story any more than at the end, because either way this would have undermined God's ability to take credit for Israel's birth as a nation.

6. See Nehama Leibowitz, *Studies in Shemot* (Jerusalem: World Zionist Organization, 1983), 149–58, drawing on Maimonides' interpretation of this issue in *Mishneh Torah*, Laws of Repentance 5:2–3.

7. See Nahum Glatzer, *Exodus, The JPS Torah Commentary* (Philadelphia: Jewish Publication Society, 1991), 23.

8. Martin Buber, "Guilt and Guilt Feelings," in *Knowledge of Man*, reprinted in *Guilt: Man and Society*, ed. Roger W. Smith (Garden City, NY: Doubleday, 1971), 102.

Part VII: *Teshuvah:* Its Moral and Spiritual Meaning

1. Max Scheler, "Repentance and Rebirth," in *On the Eternal in Man* (New York: Harper and Brothers, 1960), 55.

2. What some call "survivor guilt" I suspect is more properly identified as a feeling of having received a gift (survival despite harrowing events) that feels undeserved linked to feelings of grief (for those, frequently loved ones, who did not survive the same events).

3. Scheler, "Repentance and Rebirth," 48.

4. Ricoeur, *Symbolism of Evil*, 85.

5. Kook, *Lights of Penitence*, 54.

6. This is the provocative thesis of Jack Miles's Pulitzer Prize–winning book *God: A Biography* (New York: Vintage Books, 1995).

7. Translated by William G. Braude and Israel J. Kapstein (New York: Jewish Publication Society, 1981), 333.

8. As cited in *The Book of Legends*, ed. Hayim Nahman Bialik and Yehoshua Hana Ravnitzky, trans. William G. Braude (New York: Schocken Books, 1992), 7. See also Midrash, Psalms 90:12; Genesis Rabbah 1:4.

9. Kook, *Lights of Penitence*, 57.

10. Steinsaltz, *Strife of the Spirit*, 102.

11. Perhaps it is a prerequisite for God, too. As I noted above, the Hebrew Bible is replete with stories of God making mistakes, learning, and changing. If God, too, needs *teshuvah*, it surely must have been present before the creation of the world. I am grateful to Peter Pitzele for this intriguing (and unorthodox) suggestion.

12. Scheler, "Repentance and Rebirth," 56–57.

13. T. S. Eliot, "East Coker," in *The Complete Poems and Plays 1909–1950* (New York: Harcourt, Brace & World, 1971), 123, 129.

14. Henri Nouwen, *The Inner Voice of Love* (New York: Doubleday, 1996), 21–22.

15. Bachya ibn Pakuda dissents from this blanket statement and offers a more nuanced view of the relationship between the penitent and the wholly righteous. In his view, the penitent is on equal ground with the righteous in cases where the sin involved failure to perform a positive commandment not punishable by extirpation; the penitent is higher than the righteous when the sin was minor and the sinner repents of it completely; the righteous person is greater in cases where the sin committed is punishable by death, for in this

case atonement is only attained when the sinner dies. See *Duties of the Heart* (New York: Feldheim, 1970), 2:160–63.

16. Steinsaltz, *Strife of the Spirit*, 108–9.
17. Gershom Scholem, *The Messianic Idea in Judaism* (New York: Schocken, 1971), esp. chap. 1, "Toward an Understanding of the Messianic Idea in Judaism."
18. Peli, *Soloveitchik on Repentance*, 166.
19. In just this sense, the Christian doctrine of Christ's vicarious death and suffering, which removes the sins of humankind, is not so alien to Jewish thought as many Jews are inclined to assume.
20. Peli, *Soloveitchik on Repentance*, 77.
21. Abraham Joshua Heschel, *God in Search of Man*, 47.

Conclusion: *Teshuvah* in Our Time

1. The exceptions to this pattern are few and far between, but when they occur, they are stunning. One recent example is the statement made by U.S. Congressman Randy ("Duke") Cunningham when he resigned his office on November 28, 2005, after being indicted for fraud in connection with military contractors. His statement was a model of *teshuvah*: "When I announced several months ago that I would not seek reelection, I publicly declared my innocence because I was not strong enough to face the truth. So, I misled my family, staff, friends, colleagues, the public—even myself. For all of this, I am deeply sorry. The truth is—I broke the law, concealed my conduct, and disgraced my high office. I know that I will forfeit my freedom, my reputation, my worldly possessions, and most importantly, the trust of my friends and family.... In my life, I have known great joy and great sorrow. And now I know great shame. I learned in Viet Nam that the true measure of a man is how he responds to adversity. I cannot undo what I have done. But I can atone. I am now almost sixty-five years old, and as I enter the twilight of my life, I intend to use the remaining time that God grants me to make amends."
2. By way of example, *The Jerry Springer Show*, which features episodes in which individuals confess to having an affair with their partner's mother; see "Oops! I Cheated Again!" which aired in 2005 (*Jerry Springer*, season 14, episode 1019).
3. As of 2005, nine states—Arizona, Wyoming, Iowa, Kentucky, Alabama, Mississippi, Florida, Virginia, and Maryland—bar some or all ex-felons from voting for life, unless their rights are restored. Most, if not all, state bars and state supreme courts do not admit persons convicted of a felony to the bar. For further information on the ways in which ex-felons are excluded from many areas of public life, see Jeff Manza and Christopher Uggen, *Locked Out: Felon*

Disenfranchisement and American Democracy (New York: Oxford University Press, 2006).

4. See the *Civil Liberties Act,* Public Law 100-383, U.S. Code 50a,1989b et seq.

5. Issue 3 by President Bill Clinton on May 16, 1997.

6. On March 12, 2000, Pope John Paul II issued an apology ("Day for Pardon") for the sins of those who acted in the name of the Catholic Church. This had been preceded by a document of the International Theological Commission, *Memory and Reconciliation: The Church and the Faults of the Past.*

7. For a volume that offers religious perspectives on this approach to justice, see Michael L. Hadly, ed., *The Spiritual Roots of Restorative Justice* (Albany, NY: State University of New York Press, 2001).

Suggestions for Further Reading

Classical Sources

Albo, Joseph. *Sefer Ha-'Ikkarim (Book of Principles)*. Translated by Isaac Husik. Philadelphia: Jewish Publication Society, 1946.

Bachya ben Joseph ibn Pakuda. *Duties of the Heart*. Translated from the original Arabic by Yehuda ibn Tibbon, English translation by Moses Hyamson. New York: Feldheim, 1970. Reprinted 1986.

Cordovero, Moses. *Tomer Devorah (The Palm Tree of Deborah)*. Translated by Louis Jacobs. New York: Sepher-Hermon Press, 1960.

Jonah ben Avraham of Gerona. *The Gates of Repentance*. Translated by Shraga Silverstein. New York: Feldheim, 1971.

Kravitz, Leonard S., and Kerry M. Olitzky, eds. *The Journey of the Soul: Traditional Sources on Teshuvah*. Northvale, NJ: Jason Aronson, 1995.

Luzzatto, Moshe Chaim. *Mesilat Yesharim*. Translated and with a commentary by Yaakov Feldman. Northvale, NJ: Jason Aronson, 1996.

Maimonides, Moses. *Mishneh Torah*. "Laws of Repentance."

Orhot Tzaddikim (Ways of the Righteous). Translated by Seymour J. Cohen. New York: Feldheim, 1969. Chapter 26, "On Repentance."

Modern Sources

Borovitz, Mark. *The Holy Thief: A Con Man's Journey from Darkness to Light*. New York: HarperCollins, 2004.

Borowitz, Eugene B., and Frances Weinman Schwartz. *The Jewish Moral Virtues*. Philadelphia: Jewish Publication Society, 1999. Chapter 21, "Repentance."

Comins, Mike. *Making Prayer Real: Leading Jewish Spiritual Voices on Why Prayer Is Difficult and What to Do About It*. Woodstock, VT: Jewish Lights, 2010.

Dorff, Elliot N. *Love Your Neighbor and Yourself*. Philadelphia: Jewish Publication Society, 2003. Chapter 6, "The Elements of Forgiveness."

———. *To Do the Right and the Good: A Jewish Approach to Modern Society Ethics*. Philadelphia: Jewish Publication Society, 2002. Chapter 8, "Communal Forgiveness."

Etzioni, Amitai, ed. *Civic Repentance*. Lanham, NY: Rowman and Littlefield, 1999.

Etzioni, Amitai, and David E. Carney, eds. *Repentance: A Comparative Perspective*. Lanham, NY: Rowman and Littlefield, 1998.

Goldstein, Niles E., and Steven S. Mason. *Judaism & Spiritual Ethics*. New York: UAHC Press, 1996. "*Teshuvah*," pp. 66–74.

Hoffman, Lawrence A., ed. *Who by Fire, Who By Water—Un'taneh Tokef*. Woodstock, VT: Jewish Lights, 2010.

Kedar, Karyn D. *The Bridge to Forgiveness: Stories and Prayers for Finding God and Restoring Wholeness.* Woodstock, VT: Jewish Lights, 2007.

Kook, Abraham Isaac. *Lights of Penitence.* Translated by Ben Zion Bokser. New York: Paulist Press, 1978. Originally published in 1925.

Lazare, Aaron. *On Apology.* New York: Oxford University Press, 2004.

Milgrom, Jacob. *Numbers. The JPS Torah Commentary.* Philadelphia: Jewish Publication Society, 1990. "Repentance in the Torah and the Prophets," Excursus 22396–398.

Olitzky, Kerry M., and Rachel T. Sabath. *Striving toward Virtue.* New York: Ktav, 1996.

Olitzky, Kerry M., and Stuart A. Copans. *Twelve Jewish Steps to Recovery,* 2nd Edition: *A Personal Guide to Turning from Alcoholism and Other Addictions—Drugs, Food, Gambling, Sex ...* Woodstock, VT: Jewish Lights, 2009.

Peli, Pinchas H. *Soloveitchik on Repentance.* New York: Paulist Press, 1984.

Petuchowski, Jakob J. "Concept of *Teshuvah* in the Bible and the Talmud." *Judaism* 17 (Spring 1968): 175–85.

Schimmel, Solomon. *Wounds Not Healed by Time.* New York: Oxford University Press, 2002.

Shapiro, Rami, trans. *Ethics of the Sages:* Pirke Avot—*Annotated & Explained.* Woodstock, VT: SkyLight Paths, 2006.

———. *Recovery—The Sacred Art: The Twelve Steps as Spiritual Practice.* Woodstock, VT: SkyLight Paths, 2009.

Sherwin, Byron L. *Jewish Ethics for the Twenty-First Century.* Syracuse: Syracuse University Press, 2000. Chapter 8, "Repentance as Moral Rehabilitation."

Sherwin, Byron L., and Seymour J. Cohen. *Creating an Ethical Jewish Life: A Practical Introduction to Classic Teachings on How to Be a Jew.* Woodstock, VT: Jewish Lights, 2001.

Spitz, Elie Kaplan. *Healing from Despair: Choosing Wholeness in a Broken World.* With Erica Shapiro Taylor. Woodstock, VT: Jewish Lights, 2008.

Steinsaltz, Adin. *The Strife of the Spirit.* Northvale, NJ: Jason Aronson, 1988. Chapters 13 and 14, "*Teshuvah*" and "Repentance."

Telushkin, Joseph. *A Code of Jewish Ethics,* vol. 1. New York: Bell Tower Press, 2006. "Repentance," pp. 150–95.

Twerski, Abraham J. *A Formula for Proper Living: Practical Lessons from Life and Torah.* Woodstock, VT: Jewish Lights, 2009.

———. *Happiness and the Human Spirit: The Spirituality of Becoming the Best You Can Be.* Woodstock, VT: Jewish Lights, 2009.

Wolfson, Ron. *God's To-Do List: 103 Ways to Be an Angle and Do God's Work on Earth.* Woodstock, VT: Jewish Lights, 2006.

———. *The Seven Questions You're Asked in Heaven: Reviewing and Renewing Your Life on Earth.* Woodstock, VT: Jewish Lights, 2009.

Bible Study/Midrash

The Modern Men's Torah Commentary: New Insights from Jewish Men on the 54 Weekly Torah Portions *Edited by Rabbi Jeffrey K. Salkin*
A major contribution to modern biblical commentary. Addresses the most important concerns of modern men by opening them up to the life of Torah.
6 x 9, 368 pp, HC, 978-1-58023-395-8 **$24.99**

The Genesis of Leadership: What the Bible Teaches Us about Vision, Values and Leading Change *By Rabbi Nathan Laufer; Foreword by Senator Joseph I. Lieberman*
Unlike other books on leadership, this one is rooted in the stories of the Bible.
6 x 9, 288 pp, Quality PB, 978-1-58023-352-1 **$18.99**

Hineini in Our Lives: Learning How to Respond to Others through 14 Biblical Texts and Personal Stories *By Rabbi Norman J. Cohen, PhD* 6 x 9, 240 pp, Quality PB, 978-1-58023-274-6 **$16.99**
Moses and the Journey to Leadership: Timeless Lessons of Effective Management from the Bible and Today's Leaders *By Rabbi Norman J. Cohen, PhD*
6 x 9, 240 pp, Quality PB, 978-1-58023-351-4 **$18.99**; HC, 978-1-58023-227-2 **$21.99**
Self, Struggle & Change: Family Conflict Stories in Genesis and Their Healing Insights for Our Lives *By Rabbi Norman J. Cohen, PhD* 6 x 9, 224 pp, Quality PB, 978-1-879045-66-8 **$18.99**
The Triumph of Eve & Other Subversive Bible Tales *By Matt Biers-Ariel*
5½ x 8½, 192 pp, Quality PB, 978-1-59473-176-1 **$14.99**
(A book from SkyLight Paths, Jewish Lights' sister imprint)

The Wisdom of Judaism: An Introduction to the Values of the Talmud
By Rabbi Dov Peretz Elkins Explores the essence of Judaism through reflections on the words of the rabbinic sages. 6 x 9, 192 pp, Quality PB, 978-1-58023-327-9 **$16.99**
Also Available: **The Wisdom of Judaism Teacher's Guide**
8½ x 11, 18 pp, PB, 978-1-58023-350-7 **$8.99**

12-Step

100 Blessings Every Day: Daily Twelve Step Recovery Affirmations, Exercises for Personal Growth & Renewal Reflecting Seasons of the Jewish Year
By Rabbi Kerry M. Olitzky; Foreword by Rabbi Neil Gillman, PhD
4½ x 6½, 432 pp, Quality PB, 978-1-879045-30-9 **$16.99**

Recovery from Codependence: A Jewish Twelve Steps Guide to Healing Your Soul
By Rabbi Kerry M. Olitzky 6 x 9, 160 pp, Quality PB, 978-1-879045-32-3 **$13.95**

Twelve Jewish Steps to Recovery, 2nd Edition
A Personal Guide to Turning from Alcoholism & Other Addictions—
Drugs, Food, Gambling, Sex …
By Rabbi Kerry M. Olitzky and Stuart A. Copans, MD; Preface by Abraham J. Twerski, MD
Updated and expanded, presents a Jewish perspective on the Twelve Steps and offers consolation, inspiration and motivation for recovery by drawing on traditional and contemporary Jewish sources.
6 x 9, 160 pp, Quality PB, 978-1-58023-409-2 **$16.99**

Recovery—The Sacred Art
The Twelve Steps as Spiritual Practice
By Rabbi Rami Shapiro; Foreword by Joan Borysenko, PhD
Uniquely interprets the Twelve Steps of Alcoholics Anonymous to speak to everyone seeking a freer and more God-centered life.
5½ x 8½, 240 pp, Quality PB, 978-1-59473-259-1 **$16.99**
(A book from SkyLight Paths, Jewish Lights' sister imprint)

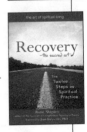

Or phone, fax, mail or e-mail to: **JEWISH LIGHTS Publishing**
Sunset Farm Offices, Route 4 • P.O. Box 237 • Woodstock, Vermont 05091
Tel: (802) 457-4000 • Fax: (802) 457-4004 • www.jewishlights.com
Credit card orders: **(800) 962-4544** (8:30AM–5:30PM ET Monday–Friday)
Generous discounts on quantity orders. SATISFACTION GUARANTEED. Prices subject to change.

Congregation Resources

Empowered Judaism: What Independent Minyanim Can Teach Us about Building Vibrant Jewish Communities
By Rabbi Elie Kaunfer; Foreword by Prof. Jonathan Sarna
Examines the independent minyan movement and what lessons these grassroots communities can provide. 6 x 9, 224 pp, Quality PB, 978-1-58023-412-2 **$18.99**

Spiritual Boredom: Rediscovering the Wonder of Judaism *By Dr. Erica Brown*
Breaks through the surface of spiritual boredom to find the reservoir of meaning within. 6 x 9, 208 pp, HC, 978-1-58023-405-4 **$21.99**

Building a Successful Volunteer Culture
Finding Meaning in Service in the Jewish Community
By Rabbi Charles Simon; Foreword by Shelley Lindauer; Preface by Dr. Ron Wolfson
Shows you how to develop and maintain the volunteers who are essential to the vitality of your organization and community. 6 x 9, 192 pp, Quality PB, 978-1-58023-408-5 **$16.99**

The Case for Jewish Peoplehood: Can We Be One?
By Dr. Erica Brown and Dr. Misha Galperin; Foreword by Rabbi Joseph Telushkin
6 x 9, 224 pp, HC, 978-1-58023-401-6 **$21.99**

Inspired Jewish Leadership: Practical Approaches to Building Strong Communities
By Dr. Erica Brown 6 x 9, 256 pp, HC, 978-1-58023-361-3 **$24.99**

Jewish Pastoral Care, 2nd Edition: A Practical Handbook from Traditional & Contemporary Sources *Edited by Rabbi Dayle A. Friedman, MSW, MAJCS, BCC*
6 x 9, 528 pp, Quality PB, 978-1-58023-427-6 **$30.00**

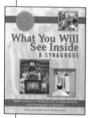

Rethinking Synagogues: A New Vocabulary for Congregational Life
By Rabbi Lawrence A. Hoffman 6 x 9, 240 pp, Quality PB, 978-1-58023-248-7 **$19.99**

The Spirituality of Welcoming: How to Transform Your Congregation into a Sacred Community *By Dr. Ron Wolfson* 6 x 9, 224 pp, Quality PB, 978-1-58023-244-9 **$19.99**

Children's Books

What You Will See Inside a Synagogue
By Rabbi Lawrence A. Hoffman, PhD, and Dr. Ron Wolfson; Full-color photos by Bill Aron
A colorful, fun-to-read introduction that explains the ways and whys of Jewish worship and religious life. 8½ x 10½, 32 pp, Full-color photos, Quality PB, 978-1-59473-256-0 **$8.99**
For ages 6 & up (A book from SkyLight Paths, Jewish Lights' sister imprint)

Because Nothing Looks Like God
By Lawrence Kushner and Karen Kushner Introduces children to the possibilities of spiritual life. 11 x 8½, 32 pp, Full-color illus., HC, 978-1-58023-092-6 **$17.99** *For ages 4 & up*
Board Book Companions to *Because Nothing Looks Like God*
5 x 5, 24 pp, Full-color illus., SkyLight Paths Board Books *For ages 0–4*
What Does God Look Like? 978-1-893361-23-2 **$7.99**
How Does God Make Things Happen? 978-1-893361-24-9 **$7.95**
Where Is God? 978-1-893361-17-1 **$7.99**

The Book of Miracles: A Young Person's Guide to Jewish Spiritual Awareness
Written and illus. by Lawrence Kushner
6 x 9, 96 pp, 2-color illus., HC, 978-1-879045-78-1 **$16.95** *For ages 9 & up*
In God's Hands
By Lawrence Kushner and Gary Schmidt 9 x 12, 32 pp, HC, 978-1-58023-224-1 **$16.99**
In Our Image: God's First Creatures *By Nancy Sohn Swartz*
9 x 12, 32 pp, Full-color illus., HC, 978-1-879045-99-6 **$16.95** *For ages 4 & up*
Also Available as a Board Book: **How Did the Animals Help God?**
5 x 5, 24 pp, Full-color illus., Board Book, 978-1-59473-044-3 **$7.99** *For ages 0–4*
(A book from SkyLight Paths, Jewish Lights' sister imprint)
The Kids' Fun Book of Jewish Time
By Emily Sper 9 x 7½, 24 pp, Full-color illus., HC, 978-1-58023-311-8 **$16.99**
What Makes Someone a Jew? *By Lauren Seidman*
Reflects the changing face of American Judaism.
10 x 8½, 32 pp, Full-color photos, Quality PB, 978-1-58023-321-7 **$8.99** *For ages 3–6*

Inspiration

The Seven Questions You're Asked in Heaven: Reviewing and Renewing Your Life on Earth *By Dr. Ron Wolfson*
An intriguing and entertaining resource for living a life that matters.
6 x 9, 176 pp, Quality PB, 978-1-58023-407-8 **$16.99**

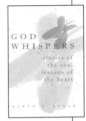

Happiness and the Human Spirit: The Spirituality of Becoming the Best You Can Be *By Abraham J. Twerski, MD*
Shows you that true happiness is attainable once you stop looking outside yourself for the source. 6 x 9, 176 pp, Quality PB, 978-1-58023-404-7 **$16.99**; HC, 978-1-58023-343-9 **$19.99**

Life's Daily Blessings: Inspiring Reflections on Gratitude and Joy for Every Day, Based on Jewish Wisdom *By Rabbi Kerry M. Olitzky* 4½ x 6½, 368 pp, Quality PB, 978-1-58023-396-5 **$16.99**

The Bridge to Forgiveness: Stories and Prayers for Finding God and Restoring Wholeness *By Rabbi Karyn D. Kedar*
Examines how forgiveness can be the bridge that connects us to wholeness and peace.
6 x 9, 176 pp, HC, 978-1-58023-324-8 **$19.99**

A Formula for Proper Living: Practical Lessons from Life and Torah
By Abraham J. Twerski, MD
Gives you practical lessons for life that you can put to day-to-day use in dealing with yourself and others. 6 x 9, 144 pp, HC, 978-1-58023-402-3 **$19.99**

God's To-Do List: 103 Ways to Be an Angel and Do God's Work on Earth
By Dr. Ron Wolfson 6 x 9, 144 pp, Quality PB, 978-1-58023-301-9 **$16.99**

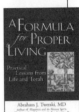

The Empty Chair: Finding Hope and Joy—Timeless Wisdom from a Hasidic Master, Rebbe Nachman of Breslov *Adapted by Moshe Mykoff and the Breslov Research Institute*
4 x 6, 128 pp, Deluxe PB w/ flaps, 978-1-879045-67-5 **$9.99**

The Gentle Weapon: Prayers for Everyday and Not-So-Everyday Moments—Timeless Wisdom from the Teachings of the Hasidic Master, Rebbe Nachman of Breslov *Adapted by Moshe Mykoff and S. C. Mizrahi, together with the Breslov Research Institute*
4 x 6, 144 pp, Deluxe PB w/ flaps, 978-1-58023-022-3 **$9.99**

God Whispers: Stories of the Soul, Lessons of the Heart *By Karyn D. Kedar*
6 x 9, 176 pp, Quality PB, 978-1-58023-088-9 **$15.95**

Restful Reflections: Nighttime Inspiration to Calm the Soul, Based on Jewish Wisdom
By Rabbi Kerry M. Olitzky and Rabbi Lori Forman 4½ x 6¼, 448 pp, Quality PB, 978-1-58023-091-9 **$15.95**

Sacred Intentions: Daily Inspiration to Strengthen the Spirit, Based on Jewish Wisdom
By Rabbi Kerry M. Olitzky and Rabbi Lori Forman 4½ x 6¼, 448 pp, Quality PB, 978-1-58023-061-2 **$15.95**

Kabbalah/Mysticism

Seek My Face: A Jewish Mystical Theology *By Arthur Green*
6 x 9, 304 pp, Quality PB, 978-1-58023-130-5 **$19.95**

Zohar: Annotated & Explained *Translation & Annotation by Daniel C. Matt; Foreword by Andrew Harvey* 5½ x 8½, 176 pp, Quality PB, 978-1-893361-51-5 **$15.99**
(A book from SkyLight Paths, Jewish Lights' sister imprint)

Ehyeh: A Kabbalah for Tomorrow
By Arthur Green 6 x 9, 224 pp, Quality PB, 978-1-58023-213-5 **$16.99**

The Flame of the Heart: Prayers of a Chasidic Mystic
By Reb Noson of Breslov; Translated and adapted by David Sears, with the Breslov Research Institute
5 x 7¼, 160 pp, Quality PB, 978-1-58023-246-3 **$15.99**

The Gift of Kabbalah: Discovering the Secrets of Heaven, Renewing Your Life on Earth
By Tamar Frankiel, PhD 6 x 9, 256 pp, Quality PB, 978-1-58023-141-1 **$16.95**

Kabbalah: A Brief Introduction for Christians
By Tamar Frankiel, PhD 5½ x 8½, 208 pp, Quality PB, 978-1-58023-303-3 **$16.99**

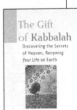

The Lost Princess & Other Kabbalistic Tales of Rebbe Nachman of Breslov
The Seven Beggars & Other Kabbalistic Tales of Rebbe Nachman of Breslov
Translated by Rabbi Aryeh Kaplan; Preface by Rabbi Chaim Kramer
Lost Princess: 6 x 9, 400 pp, Quality PB, 978-1-58023-217-3 **$18.99**
Seven Beggars: 6 x 9, 192 pp, Quality PB, 978-1-58023-250-0 **$16.99**

See also *The Way Into Jewish Mystical Tradition* in The Way Into... Series.

Social Justice

There Shall Be No Needy
Pursuing Social Justice through Jewish Law and Tradition
By Rabbi Jill Jacobs; Foreword by Rabbi Elliot N. Dorff, PhD; Preface by Simon Greer
Confronts the most pressing issues of twenty-first-century America from a deeply Jewish perspective.
6 x 9, 288 pp, Quality PB, 978-1-58023-425-2 **$16.99**; HC, 978-1-58023-394-1 **$21.99**

Conscience: The Duty to Obey and the Duty to Disobey
By Rabbi Harold M. Schulweis
This clarion call to rethink our moral and political behavior examines the idea of conscience and the role conscience plays in our relationships to governments, law, ethics, religion, human nature, God—and to each other.
6 x 9, 160 pp, Quality PB, 978-1-58023-419-1 **$16.99**; HC, 978-1-58023-375-0 **$19.99**

Judaism and Justice: The Jewish Passion to Repair the World
By Rabbi Sidney Schwarz; Foreword by Ruth Messinger
Explores the relationship between Judaism, social justice and the Jewish identity of American Jews.
6 x 9, 352 pp, Quality PB, 978-1-58023-353-8 **$19.99**; HC, 978-1-58023-312-5 **$24.99**

Spiritual Activism: A Jewish Guide to Leadership and Repairing the World
By Rabbi Avraham Weiss; Foreword by Alan M. Dershowitz
6 x 9, 224 pp, Quality PB, 978-1-58023-418-4 **$16.99**; HC, 978-1-58023-355-2 **$24.99**

Righteous Indignation: A Jewish Call for Justice
Edited by Rabbi Or N. Rose, Jo Ellen Green Kaiser and Margie Klein; Foreword by Rabbi David Ellenson
Leading progressive Jewish activists explore meaningful intellectual and spiritual foundations for their social justice work.
6 x 9, 384 pp, Quality PB, 978-1-58023-414-6 **$19.99**; HC, 978-1-58023-336-1 **$24.99**

Spirituality/Women's Interest

New Jewish Feminism: Probing the Past, Forging the Future
Edited by Rabbi Elyse Goldstein; Foreword by Anita Diamant
Looks at the growth and accomplishments of Jewish feminism and what they mean for Jewish women today and tomorrow.
6 x 9, 480 pp, HC, 978-1-58023-359-0 **$24.99**

The Quotable Jewish Woman: Wisdom, Inspiration & Humor from the Mind & Heart
Edited by Elaine Bernstein Partnow
6 x 9, 496 pp, Quality PB, 978-1-58023-236-4 **$19.99**

The Divine Feminine in Biblical Wisdom Literature
Selections Annotated & Explained
Translated and Annotated by Rabbi Rami Shapiro
5½ x 8½, 240 pp, Quality PB, 978-1-59473-109-9 **$16.99**
(A book from SkyLight Paths, Jewish Lights' sister imprint)

The Women's Haftarah Commentary: New Insights from Women Rabbis on the 54 Weekly Haftarah Portions, the 5 Megillot & Special Shabbatot
Edited by Rabbi Elyse Goldstein
Illuminates the historical significance of female portrayals in the Haftarah and the Five Megillot.
6 x 9, 560 pp, Quality PB, 978-1-58023-371-2 **$19.99**; HC, 978-1-58023-133-6 **$39.99**

The Women's Torah Commentary: New Insights from Women Rabbis on the 54 Weekly Torah Portions
Edited by Rabbi Elyse Goldstein
Over fifty women rabbis offer inspiring insights on the Torah, in a week-by-week format.
6 x 9, 496 pp, Quality PB, 978-1-58023-370-5 **$19.99**; HC, 978-1-58023-076-6 **$34.95**

See Passover for *The Women's Passover Companion: Women's Reflections on the Festival of Freedom* and *The Women's Seder Sourcebook: Rituals & Readings for Use at the Passover Seder.*

Spirituality/Lawrence Kushner

The Book of Letters: A Mystical Hebrew Alphabet
Popular HC Edition, 6 x 9, 80 pp, 2-color text, 978-1-879045-00-2 **$24.95**
Collector's Limited Edition, 9 x 12, 80 pp, gold-foil-embossed pages, w/ limited-edition silkscreened
print, 978-1-879045-04-0 **$349.00**

The Book of Miracles: A Young Person's Guide to Jewish Spiritual Awareness
6 x 9, 96 pp, 2-color illus., HC, 978-1-879045-78-1 **$16.95** *For ages 9–13*

The Book of Words: Talking Spiritual Life, Living Spiritual Talk
6 x 9, 160 pp, Quality PB, 978-1-58023-020-9 **$16.95**

Eyes Remade for Wonder: A Lawrence Kushner Reader *Introduction by Thomas Moore*
6 x 9, 240 pp, Quality PB, 978-1-58023-042-1 **$18.95**

Filling Words with Light: Hasidic and Mystical Reflections on Jewish Prayer
By Rabbi Lawrence Kushner and Rabbi Nehemia Polen
5½ x 8½, 176 pp, Quality PB, 978-1-58023-238-8 **$16.99**; HC, 978-1-58023-216-6 **$21.99**

God Was in This Place & I, i Did Not Know: Finding Self, Spirituality and
Ultimate Meaning 6 x 9, 192 pp, Quality PB, 978-1-879045-33-0 **$16.95**

Honey from the Rock: An Introduction to Jewish Mysticism
6 x 9, 176 pp, Quality PB, 978-1-58023-073-5 **$16.95**

Invisible Lines of Connection: Sacred Stories of the Ordinary
5½ x 8½, 160 pp, Quality PB, 978-1-879045-98-9 **$15.95**

Jewish Spirituality: A Brief Introduction for Christians
5½ x 8½, 112 pp, Quality PB, 978-1-58023-150-3 **$12.95**

The River of Light: Jewish Mystical Awareness
6 x 9, 192 pp, Quality PB, 978-1-58023-096-4 **$16.95**

The Way Into Jewish Mystical Tradition
6 x 9, 224 pp, Quality PB, 978-1-58023-200-5 **$18.99**; HC, 978-1-58023-029-2 **$21.95**

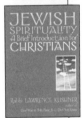

Spirituality/Prayer

Making Prayer Real: Leading Jewish Spiritual Voices on Why Prayer Is
Difficult and What to Do about It *By Rabbi Mike Comins*
A no-holds-barred look at why so many find synagogue at best difficult, and at
worst, meaningless and boring—and how to make it more satisfying.
6 x 9, 288 pp, Quality PB, 978-1-58023-417-7 **$18.99**

Witnesses to the One: The Spiritual History of the *Sh'ma By Rabbi Joseph B. Meszler;*
Foreword by Rabbi Elyse Goldstein 6 x 9, 176 pp, Quality PB, 978-1-58023-400-9 **$16.99**;
HC, 978-1-58023-309-5 **$19.99**

My People's Prayer Book Series: Traditional Prayers, Modern
Commentaries *Edited by Rabbi Lawrence A. Hoffman, PhD*
Provides diverse and exciting commentary to the traditional liturgy. Will help you
find new wisdom in Jewish prayer, and bring liturgy into your life. Each book
includes Hebrew text, modern translation and commentaries from all perspectives
of the Jewish world.

Vol. 1—The *Sh'ma* and Its Blessings
   7 x 10, 168 pp, HC, 978-1-879045-79-8 **$24.99**
Vol. 2—The *Amidah* 7 x 10, 240 pp, HC, 978-1-879045-80-4 **$24.95**
Vol. 3—*P'sukei D'zimrah* (Morning Psalms)
   7 x 10, 240 pp, HC, 978-1-879045-81-1 **$24.95**
Vol. 4—*Seder K'riat Hatorah* (The Torah Service)
   7 x 10, 264 pp, HC, 978-1-879045-82-8 **$23.95**
Vol. 5—*Birkhot Hashachar* (Morning Blessings)
   7 x 10, 240 pp, HC, 978-1-879045-83-5 **$24.95**
Vol. 6—*Tachanun* and Concluding Prayers
   7 x 10, 240 pp, HC, 978-1-879045-84-2 **$24.95**
Vol. 7—Shabbat at Home 7 x 10, 240 pp, HC, 978-1-879045-85-9 **$24.95**
Vol. 8—*Kabbalat Shabbat* (Welcoming Shabbat in the Synagogue)
   7 x 10, 240 pp, HC, 978-1-58023-121-3 **$24.99**
Vol. 9—Welcoming the Night: *Minchah* and *Ma'ariv* (Afternoon and
   Evening Prayer) 7 x 10, 272 pp, HC, 978-1-58023-262-3 **$24.99**
Vol. 10—Shabbat Morning: *Shacharit* and *Musaf* (Morning and
   Additional Services) 7 x 10, 240 pp, HC, 978-1-58023-240-1 **$24.99**

Spirituality

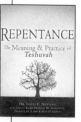

Repentance: The Meaning and Practice of *Teshuvah*
By Dr. Louis E. Newman; Foreword by Rabbi Harold M. Schulweis; Preface by Rabbi Karyn D. Kedar
Examines both the practical and philosophical dimensions of *teshuvah*, Judaism's core religious-moral teaching on repentance, and its value for us—Jews and non-Jews alike—today. 6 x 9, 256 pp, HC, 978-1-58023-426-9 **$24.99**

Tanya, the Masterpiece of Hasidic Wisdom
Selections Annotated & Explained
Translation & Annotation by Rabbi Rami Shapiro
Brings the genius of the *Tanya* to anyone seeking to deepen their understanding of the soul and how it relates to and manifests the Divine Source.
5½ x 8½, 192 pp (est), Quality PB, 978-1-59473-275-1 **$16.99**
(A book from SkyLight Paths, Jewish Lights' sister imprint)

A Book of Life: Embracing Judaism as a Spiritual Practice
By Rabbi Michael Strassfeld 6 x 9, 544 pp, Quality PB, 978-1-58023-247-0 **$19.99**

Meaning and Mitzvah: Daily Practices for Reclaiming Judaism through Prayer, God, Torah, Hebrew, Mitzvot and Peoplehood By Rabbi Goldie Milgram
7 x 9, 336 pp, Quality PB, 978-1-58023-256-2 **$19.99**

The Soul of the Story: Meetings with Remarkable People
By Rabbi David Zeller 6 x 9, 288 pp, HC, 978-1-58023-272-2 **$21.99**

Aleph-Bet Yoga: Embodying the Hebrew Letters for Physical and Spiritual Well-Being
By Steven A. Rapp; Foreword by Tamar Frankiel, PhD, and Judy Greenfeld; Preface by Hart Lazer
7 x 10, 128 pp, b/w photos, Quality PB, Layflat binding, 978-1-58023-162-6 **$16.95**

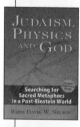

Does the Soul Survive? A Jewish Journey to Belief in Afterlife, Past Lives & Living with Purpose By Rabbi Elie Kaplan Spitz; Foreword by Brian L. Weiss, MD
6 x 9, 288 pp, Quality PB, 978-1-58023-165-7 **$16.99**

First Steps to a New Jewish Spirit: Reb Zalman's Guide to Recapturing the Intimacy & Ecstasy in Your Relationship with God By Rabbi Zalman M. Schachter-Shalomi with Donald Gropman 6 x 9, 144 pp, Quality PB, 978-1-58023-182-4 **$16.95**

Foundations of Sephardic Spirituality: The Inner Life of Jews of the Ottoman Empire
By Rabbi Marc D. Angel, PhD 6 x 9, 224 pp, Quality PB, 978-1-58023-341-5 **$18.99**

God in Our Relationships: Spirituality between People from the Teachings of Martin Buber By Rabbi Dennis S. Ross 5½ x 8½, 160 pp, Quality PB, 978-1-58023-147-3 **$16.95**

Judaism, Physics and God: Searching for Sacred Metaphors in a Post-Einstein World
By Rabbi David W. Nelson 6 x 9, 352 pp, Quality PB, inc. reader's discussion guide,
978-1-58023-306-4 **$18.99**; HC, 352 pp, 978-1-58023-252-4 **$24.99**

The Jewish Lights Spirituality Handbook: A Guide to Understanding, Exploring & Living a Spiritual Life Edited by Stuart M. Matlins
What exactly is "Jewish" about spirituality? How do I make it a part of my life? Fifty of today's foremost spiritual leaders share their ideas and experience with us.
6 x 9, 456 pp, Quality PB, 978-1-58023-093-3 **$19.99**

Bringing the Psalms to Life: How to Understand and Use the Book of Psalms
By Rabbi Daniel F. Polish, PhD 6 x 9, 208 pp, Quality PB, 978-1-58023-157-2 **$16.95**

God & the Big Bang: Discovering Harmony between Science & Spirituality
By Dr. Daniel C. Matt 6 x 9, 216 pp, Quality PB, 978-1-879045-89-7 **$16.99**

Minding the Temple of the Soul: Balancing Body, Mind, and Spirit through Traditional Jewish Prayer, Movement, and Meditation By Tamar Frankiel, PhD, and Judy Greenfeld
7 x 10, 184 pp, illus., Quality PB, 978-1-879045-64-4 **$16.95**

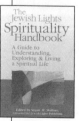

One God Clapping: The Spiritual Path of a Zen Rabbi By Alan Lew with Sherril Jaffe
5½ x 8½, 336 pp, Quality PB, 978-1-58023-115-2 **$16.95**

There Is No Messiah ... and You're It: The Stunning Transformation of Judaism's Most Provocative Idea By Rabbi Robert N. Levine, DD
6 x 9, 192 pp, Quality PB, 978-1-58023-255-5 **$16.95**

These Are the Words: A Vocabulary of Jewish Spiritual Life
By Rabbi Arthur Green, PhD 6 x 9, 304 pp, Quality PB, 978-1-58023-107-7 **$18.95**

Holidays/Holy Days

Who By Fire, Who By Water—Un'taneh Tokef
Edited by Rabbi Lawrence A. Hoffman, PhD
Examines the prayer's theology, authorship and poetry through a set of lively essays, all written in accessible language.
6 x 9, 304 pp (est), HC, 978-1-58023-424-5 **$24.99**

Rosh Hashanah Readings: Inspiration, Information and Contemplation
Yom Kippur Readings: Inspiration, Information and Contemplation
Edited by Rabbi Dov Peretz Elkins; Section Introductions from Arthur Green's These Are the Words
An extraordinary collection of readings, prayers and insights that will enable you to enter into the spirit of the High Holy Days in a personal and powerful way, permitting the meaning of the Jewish New Year to enter the heart.
Rosh Hashanah: 6 x 9, 400 pp, HC, 978-1-58023-239-5 **$24.99**
Yom Kippur: 6 x 9, 368 pp, HC, 978-1-58023-271-5 **$24.99**

Jewish Holidays: A Brief Introduction for Christians
By Rabbi Kerry M. Olitzky and Rabbi Daniel Judson
5½ x 8½, 176 pp, Quality PB, 978-1-58023-302-6 **$16.99**

Reclaiming Judaism as a Spiritual Practice: Holy Days and Shabbat
By Rabbi Goldie Milgram 7 x 9, 272 pp, Quality PB, 978-1-58023-205-0 **$19.99**

7th Heaven: Celebrating Shabbat with Rebbe Nachman of Breslov
By Moshe Mykoff with the Breslov Research Institute
5⅛ x 8¼, 224 pp, Deluxe PB w/ flaps, 978-1-58023-175-6 **$18.95**

Shabbat, 2nd Edition: The Family Guide to Preparing for and Celebrating
the Sabbath By Dr. Ron Wolfson
7 x 9, 320 pp, illus., Quality PB, 978-1-58023-164-0 **$19.99**

Hanukkah, 2nd Edition: The Family Guide to Spiritual Celebration
By Dr. Ron Wolfson 7 x 9, 240 pp, illus., Quality PB, 978-1-58023-122-0 **$18.95**

The Jewish Family Fun Book, 2nd Edition: Holiday Projects, Everyday Activities,
and Travel Ideas with Jewish Themes By Danielle Dardashti and Roni Sarig; Illus. by Avi Katz
6 x 9, 304 pp, 70+ b/w illus. & diagrams, Quality PB, 978-1-58023-333-0 **$18.99**

The Jewish Lights Book of Fun Classroom Activities: Simple and Seasonal
Projects for Teachers and Students By Danielle Dardashti and Roni Sarig
6 x 9, 240 pp, Quality PB, 978-1-58023-206-7 **$19.99**

Passover

My People's Passover Haggadah
Traditional Texts, Modern Commentaries
Edited by Rabbi Lawrence A. Hoffman, PhD, and David Arnow, PhD
A diverse and exciting collection of commentaries on the traditional Passover Haggadah—in two volumes!
Vol. 1: 7 x 10, 304 pp, HC, 978-1-58023-354-5 **$24.99**
Vol. 2: 7 x 10, 320 pp, HC, 978-1-58023-346-0 **$24.99**

Leading the Passover Journey: The Seder's Meaning Revealed, the
Haggadah's Story Retold By Rabbi Nathan Laufer
Uncovers the hidden meaning of the Seder's rituals and customs.
6 x 9, 224 pp, Quality PB, 978-1-58023-399-6 **$18.99**; HC, 978-1-58023-211-1 **$24.99**

The Women's Passover Companion: Women's Reflections on the Festival of Freedom
Edited by Rabbi Sharon Cohen Anisfeld, Tara Mohr and Catherine Spector; Foreword by Paula E. Hyman
6 x 9, 352 pp, Quality PB, 978-1-58023-231-9 **$19.99**

The Women's Seder Sourcebook: Rituals & Readings for Use at the Passover Seder
Edited by Rabbi Sharon Cohen Anisfeld, Tara Mohr and Catherine Spector; Foreword by Paula E. Hyman
6 x 9, 384 pp, Quality PB, 978-1-58023-232-6 **$19.99**

Creating Lively Passover Seders: A Sourcebook of Engaging Tales, Texts & Activities
By David Arnow, PhD 7 x 9, 416 pp, Quality PB, 978-1-58023-184-8 **$24.99**

Passover, 2nd Edition: The Family Guide to Spiritual Celebration
By Dr. Ron Wolfson with Joel Lurie Grishaver 7 x 9, 352 pp, Quality PB, 978-1-58023-174-9 **$19.95**

Theology/Philosophy/The Way Into... Series

The Way Into... series offers an accessible and highly usable "guided tour" of the Jewish faith, people, history and beliefs—in total, an introduction to Judaism that will enable you to understand and interact with the sacred texts of the Jewish tradition. Each volume is written by a leading contemporary scholar and teacher, and explores one key aspect of Judaism. The Way Into... series enables all readers to achieve a real sense of Jewish cultural literacy through guided study.

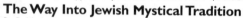

The Way Into Encountering God in Judaism
By Rabbi Neil Gillman, PhD
For everyone who wants to understand how Jews have encountered God throughout history and today.
6 x 9, 240 pp, Quality PB, 978-1-58023-199-2 **$18.99**; HC, 978-1-58023-025-4 **$21.95**
Also Available: **The Jewish Approach to God:** A Brief Introduction for Christians
By Rabbi Neil Gillman, PhD
5¼ x 8¼, 192 pp, Quality PB, 978-1-58023-190-9 **$16.95**

The Way Into Jewish Mystical Tradition
By Rabbi Lawrence Kushner
Allows readers to interact directly with the sacred mystical texts of the Jewish tradition. An accessible introduction to the concepts of Jewish mysticism, their religious and spiritual significance, and how they relate to life today.
6 x 9, 224 pp, Quality PB, 978-1-58023-200-5 **$18.99**; HC, 978-1-58023-029-2 **$21.95**

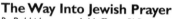

The Way Into Jewish Prayer
By Rabbi Lawrence A. Hoffman, PhD
Opens the door to 3,000 years of Jewish prayer, making available all anyone needs to feel at home in the Jewish way of communicating with God.
6 x 9, 208 pp, Quality PB, 978-1-58023-201-2 **$18.99**

Also Available: **The Way Into Jewish Prayer Teacher's Guide**
By Rabbi Jennifer Ossakow Goldsmith
8½ x 11, 42 pp, PB, 978-1-58023-345-3 **$8.99**
Download a free copy at www.jewishlights.com.

The Way Into Judaism and the Environment
By Jeremy Benstein, PhD
Explores the ways in which Judaism contributes to contemporary social-environmental issues, the extent to which Judaism is part of the problem and how it can be part of the solution.
6 x 9, 288 pp, Quality PB, 978-1-58023-368-2 **$18.99**; HC, 978-1-58023-268-5 **$24.99**

The Way Into Tikkun Olam (Repairing the World)
By Rabbi Elliot N. Dorff, PhD
An accessible introduction to the Jewish concept of the individual's responsibility to care for others and repair the world.
6 x 9, 304 pp, Quality PB, 978-1-58023-328-6 **$18.99**; 320 pp, HC, 978-1-58023-269-2 **$24.99**

The Way Into Torah
By Rabbi Norman J. Cohen, PhD
Helps guide in the exploration of the origins and development of Torah, explains why it should be studied and how to do it.
6 x 9, 176 pp, Quality PB, 978-1-58023-198-5 **$16.99**

The Way Into the Varieties of Jewishness
By Sylvia Barack Fishman, PhD
Explores the religious and historical understanding of what it has meant to be Jewish from ancient times to the present controversy over "Who is a Jew?"
6 x 9, 288 pp, Quality PB, 978-1-58023-367-5 **$18.99**; HC, 978-1-58023-030-8 **$24.99**

Theology/Philosophy

Jewish Theology in Our Time: A New Generation Explores the Foundations and Future of Jewish Belief *Edited by Rabbi Elliot J. Cosgrove, PhD* A powerful and challenging examination of what Jews can believe—by a new generation's most dynamic and innovative thinkers.
6 x 9, 350 pp (est), HC, 978-1-58023-413-9 **$24.99**

Maimonides, Spinoza and Us: Toward an Intellectually Vibrant Judaism
By Rabbi Marc D. Angel, PhD A challenging look at two great Jewish philosophers, and what their thinking means to our understanding of God, truth, revelation and reason. 6 x 9, 224 pp, HC, 978-1-58023-411-5 **$24.99**

A Touch of the Sacred: A Theologian's Informal Guide to Jewish Belief
By Dr. Eugene B. Borowitz and Frances W. Schwartz
Explores the musings from the leading theologian of liberal Judaism.
6 x 9, 256 pp, Quality PB, 978-1-58023-416-0 **$16.99**; HC, 978-1-58023-337-8 **$21.99**

Jews and Judaism in the 21st Century: Human Responsibility, the Presence of God, and the Future of the Covenant *Edited by Rabbi Edward Feinstein; Foreword by Paula E. Hyman* Five celebrated leaders in Judaism examine contemporary Jewish life. 6 x 9, 192 pp, Quality PB, 978-1-58023-374-3 **$19.99**; HC, 978-1-58023-315-6 **$24.99**

The Death of Death: Resurrection and Immortality in Jewish Thought
By Rabbi Neil Gillman, PhD 6 x 9, 336 pp, Quality PB, 978-1-58023-081-0 **$18.95**

Ethics of the Sages: *Pirke Avot*—Annotated & Explained
Translation & Annotation by Rabbi Rami Shapiro
5½ x 8½, 192 pp, Quality PB, 978-1-59473-207-2 **$16.99** (A book from SkyLight Paths, Jewish Lights' sister imprint)

Hasidic Tales: Annotated & Explained *Translation & Annotation by Rabbi Rami Shapiro*
5½ x 8½, 240 pp, Quality PB, 978-1-893361-86-7 **$16.95** (A book from SkyLight Paths, Jewish Lights' sister imprint)

A Heart of Many Rooms: Celebrating the Many Voices within Judaism
By Dr. David Hartman 6 x 9, 352 pp, Quality PB, 978-1-58023-156-5 **$19.95**

The Hebrew Prophets: Selections Annotated & Explained
Translation & Annotation by Rabbi Rami Shapiro; Foreword by Rabbi Zalman M. Schachter-Shalomi
5½ x 8½, 224 pp, Quality PB, 978-1-59473-037-5 **$16.99** (A book from SkyLight Paths, Jewish Lights' sister imprint)

A Jewish Understanding of the New Testament
By Rabbi Samuel Sandmel; Preface by Rabbi David Sandmel
5½ x 8½, 368 pp, Quality PB, 978-1-59473-048-1 **$19.99** (A book from SkyLight Paths, Jewish Lights' sister imprint)

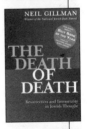

Keeping Faith with the Psalms: Deepen Your Relationship with God Using the Book of Psalms *By Rabbi Daniel F. Polish, PhD* 6 x 9, 320 pp, Quality PB, 978-1-58023-300-2 **$18.99**

A Living Covenant: The Innovative Spirit in Traditional Judaism
By Dr. David Hartman 6 x 9, 368 pp, Quality PB, 978-1-58023-011-7 **$20.00**

Love and Terror in the God Encounter: The Theological Legacy of Rabbi Joseph B. Soloveitchik *By Dr. David Hartman* 6 x 9, 240 pp, Quality PB, 978-1-58023-176-3 **$19.95**

The Personhood of God: Biblical Theology, Human Faith and the Divine Image
By Dr. Yochanan Muffs; Foreword by Dr. David Hartman
6 x 9, 240 pp, Quality PB, 978-1-58023-338-5 **$18.99**; HC, 978-1-58023-265-4 **$24.99**

Traces of God: Seeing God in Torah, History and Everyday Life *By Rabbi Neil Gillman, PhD*
6 x 9, 240 pp, Quality PB, 978-1-58023-369-9 **$16.99**; HC, 978-1-58023-249-4 **$21.99**

We Jews and Jesus: Exploring Theological Differences for Mutual Understanding
By Rabbi Samuel Sandmel; Preface by Rabbi David Sandmel
6 x 9, 192 pp, Quality PB, 978-1-59473-208-9 **$16.99** (A book from SkyLight Paths, Jewish Lights' sister imprint)

Your Word Is Fire: The Hasidic Masters on Contemplative Prayer
Edited and translated by Rabbi Arthur Green, PhD, and Barry W. Holtz
6 x 9, 160 pp, Quality PB, 978-1-879045-25-5 **$15.95**

I Am Jewish
Personal Reflections Inspired by the Last Words of Daniel Pearl
Almost 150 Jews—both famous and not—from all walks of life, from all around the world, write about many aspects of their Judaism.
Edited by Judea and Ruth Pearl 6 x 9, 304 pp, Deluxe PB w/ flaps, 978-1-58023-259-3 **$18.99**
Download a free copy of the *I Am Jewish Teacher's Guide* at www.jewishlights.com.

About Jewish Lights

People of all faiths and backgrounds yearn for books that attract, engage, educate, and spiritually inspire.

Our principal goal is to stimulate thought and help all people learn about who the Jewish People are, where they come from, and what the future can be made to hold. While people of our diverse Jewish heritage are the primary audience, our books speak to people in the Christian world as well and will broaden their understanding of Judaism and the roots of their own faith.

We bring to you authors who are at the forefront of spiritual thought and experience. While each has something different to say, they all say it in a voice that you can hear.

Our books are designed to welcome you and then to engage, stimulate, and inspire. We judge our success not only by whether or not our books are beautiful and commercially successful, but by whether or not they make a difference in your life.

For your information and convenience, at the back of this book we have provided a list of other Jewish Lights books you might find interesting and useful. They cover all the categories of your life:

Bar/Bat Mitzvah	Life Cycle
Bible Study / Midrash	Meditation
Children's Books	Men's Interest
Congregation Resources	Parenting
Current Events / History	Prayer / Ritual / Sacred Practice
Ecology / Environment	Social Justice
Fiction: Mystery, Science Fiction	Spirituality
Grief / Healing	Theology / Philosophy
Holidays / Holy Days	Travel
Inspiration	12-Step
Kabbalah / Mysticism / Enneagram	Women's Interest

Stuart M. Matlins, Publisher

Or phone, fax, mail or e-mail to: **JEWISH LIGHTS Publishing**
Sunset Farm Offices, Route 4 • P.O. Box 237 • Woodstock, Vermont 05091
Tel: (802) 457-4000 • Fax: (802) 457-4004 • www.jewishlights.com
Credit card orders: **(800) 962-4544** (8:30AM–5:30PM ET Monday–Friday)
Generous discounts on quantity orders. SATISFACTION GUARANTEED. Prices subject to change.